VEGAN

NORTH

A CELEBRATION OF THE AMAZING VEGAN
FOOD & DRINK IN THE NORTH OF ENGLAND

VEGAN
NORTH

First edition printed in 2019 in the UK
ISBN: 978-1-910863-40-4

Thank you: Simon Rimmer, Greens

Compiled by: Anna Tebble

Written by: Katie Fisher

Photography by:
Marc Barker, Matt Crowder,
Tim Green, Carl Sukonik

Designed by: Paul Cocker

Edited by: Katie Fisher, Phil Turner

Contributors: Ruth Alexander,
Vanesa Balaj, Amelia Brownhill,
Sarah Koriba, Jo Mallinder,
Lauren Nuttall, Paul Stimpson,
David Wilson

Published by Meze Publishing Limited
Unit 1b, 2 Kelham Square
Kelham Riverside
Sheffield S3 8SD

Web: www.mezepublishing.co.uk

Telephone: 0114 275 7709

Email: info@mezepublishing.co.uk

Printed in the UK by Bell & Bain Ltd

FOREWORD

Simon Connolly and I opened Greens in 1990 with little knowledge, ability or business acumen, but with bagfuls of passion and a desire to learn.

Originally, Greens was a 28 cover BYO vegetarian restaurant. We got AA listed, Good Food Guide listed as well as winning other awards and had a national profile. Now, 28 years later, we're up to 84 covers. We kind of know a bit more than we did then, but the passion and love for what we do has increased not decreased.

Over the years the food has developed and changed. In the last three years we've become excited, to the brink of obsession, about vegan food. We've always had a few vegan dishes on the menu, but now we're about 75% vegan on everything except desserts. The modern vegan customer wants exciting, funky dishes. It's a great challenge to a chef. We try and have the least human intervention in our food, so you won't find vegan 'chicken' nuggets on the menu. Tenderstem katsu, vegan gnocchi with pesto, Moroccan spiced and stuffed aubergine as well as vegan cheesecake and a delicious chocolate and avocado mousse will however be featured!

The North West has a tremendously creative and progressive food and drink industry, and it's joyous to see not only great veggie but also great vegan dishes popping up all over menus. Restaurateurs and customers alike are excited about this whole new world of dishes. Chefs are retraining to learn about meat and dairy-free options, this time excited by the possibilities rather than thinking that a dry and tasteless mushroom risotto will do.

This book celebrates exactly that premise, with good stories and great recipes from a part of the industry that is definitely the future.

SIMON RIMMER

WELCOME TO VEGAN NORTH

Long gone are the days when being a vegan meant having to choose between a single option on a restaurant menu or not eating out at all. The unstoppable rise of veganism in recent years has led to an influx of plant-based eateries that offer innovative and delicious food, where meat is no longer the star.

We have searched the North of England to find the best restaurants, cafés, small producers that are pioneers of this thriving vegan food scene. Taking a tour from Manchester and Liverpool through Sheffield and up to Newcastle, this book showcases recipes and stories right across the region devoted to challenging pre-conceived stereotypes about plant-based cooking. Far from bland and unimaginative, their recipes vary from vegan twists on regional classics to exotic concoctions, each one simple enough to be cooked and enjoyed at home. From established eateries such as Eighth Day in Manchester to rising stars Make No Bones in Sheffield, each business featured plays a part in representing the diverse, inventive and above all fun nature of the northern vegan food scene.

Whether you are a practicing vegan, a recent convert or simply interested in finding out more about the possibilities of vegan cooking, this book is one to learn from, whether it's to find new plant-based hotspots, or use these recipes as inspiration for your own culinary creations. Plant-powered and proud, this book is an exciting glimpse into the future of northern cuisine, more vibrant and diverse than ever before.

CONTENTS

BUND OR
BUST

Calling all vegans in Leeds, Manchester and Liverpool: what's not to love about the pairing of great beer and authentic Indian street food?

Bundobust came into being thanks to a combination of far-reaching vision and happy chance. Co-owners Mark and Mayur initially had separate businesses; a small beer bar in Bradford and a vegan and vegetarian Indian restaurant in West Yorkshire respectively. Mayur's family ran Prashad, the restaurant, and invited Mark to do a beer and food matching event there, which proved so popular that it seemed remiss not to make more of it. Mayur and Mark began with pop-ups and appeared at food festivals with Indian street food and craft beer that went down a treat.

Their growing fan base got some very exciting news in July 2014, when the first Bundobust restaurant opened in Leeds. Manchester was the obvious choice for the next venue two years later, where they were visited by restaurant critic Jay Rayner. He wrote a review in The Observer that put Bundobust on the map nationally as well as regionally, and in Spring 2019 the next venue opened in Liverpool on a street full of other independents. It's a place that "fits the vibe" of the expanding group, which is important to the co-owners.

Each venue embodies Bundobust's recognisable style, but has plenty of individuality, with original features such as an atrium in Leeds and Victorian glazed tiles in Manchester. The spiritual home of every Bundobust, though, is the Gujarat region of India which, along with recipes from Mayur's family, inspires the traditional dishes on the menu. Seasonal specials combine UK produce with lashings of subcontinental spice, but favourites such as okra fries – coated in chickpea batter, deep fried, dusted with black salt and mango powder – and bhel puri are available year-round.

To wash it all down, Bundobust serve the best of international and local craft beers and have done lots of collaborations to produce unique beverages with Northern breweries. Their impressive line-up will soon include Bundobust's own 100% vegan beer; the next big project pencilled in for the thriving company is a second Manchester venue complete with brewing facilities. As Jay Rayner pointed out, it's a mystery why nobody put Indian street food and craft beer together sooner, but Bundobust have made this perfect pairing completely their own.

BUNDOBUST

INDIAN STREET FOOD   CRAFT BEER

OKRA FRIES
BUNDOBUST

BUNDOBUST
WELCOME PLEASE

BUNDOBUST

BUNDOBUST
CHOLE SAAG

Chole or chana saag is a classic Indian curry made with chickpeas and spinach. Hearty and warming, but quick enough to make on a weeknight, this is a delicious dish full of aromatic flavour.

30ml vegetable or rapeseed oil

½ tsp cumin seeds

1 tbsp garam masala

½ cinnamon stick

1 black cardamom pod

1 star anise

2 large onions, chopped

2½cm piece of ginger

3 green chillies

½ tbsp ground coriander

½ tbsp ground cumin

½ tbsp turmeric

1 tin of chopped tomatoes

3 tins of chickpeas, drained

1 tbsp salt

3 bags of spinach

Put the oil into a large pan on a high heat, and add the cumin seeds, garam masala, cinnamon, cardamom and star anise. Cook for 1 minute to release the oils from the spices but don't allow them to burn. Blend the onions to a fine paste, add to the pan and brown for 10 minutes on a medium heat.

Chop the ginger and chillies and add them to the pan. Cook for 2 minutes then add the rest of the spices (ground coriander, ground cumin and turmeric).

Next add the tinned tomatoes then fill the tin three quarters full with water and add to the pot. Bring to a simmer and add the drained chickpeas. Boil for 10 minutes then add the salt. Meanwhile, blend half of the spinach and roughly chop the other half.

After the chickpeas have been boiled for 10 minutes, add the blended spinach and mix through. Turn the heat down to a simmer and cook for a further 3 minutes. Then turn off the heat. Add the other half of the spinach and put the lid on. It's ready to serve as soon as the spinach has wilted and been stirred through.

Check the seasoning and garnish with freshly chopped coriander. Best served with puri but equally good with boiled basmati rice.

FOOD FOR
THOUGHT

The Buddhist principles behind Dana – a coffee house and vegetarian café in Crookes, Sheffield – have created an atmosphere, environment and menu that people want to return for time and again.

Vegan and vegetarian breakfast and lunch is always the order of the day at Dana, the coffee house and café in Sheffield which serves delicious food and drink sourced ethically and locally. Alongside the morally conscious menu, the atmosphere at Dana really sets it apart. The venue in Crookes was fully refurbished with warm wood panelling, clean white walls and bright splashes of yellow and turquoise to make the light-filled space homely and welcoming. Plenty of greenery also contributes to a very calming environment, encouraged and maintained by the team of people running the café cooperatively: Jenny, Dajavajra, Maitridasa and Amalasiddhi.

Dana opened in May 2017 following a unique journey towards its realisation. A group of friends and fellow Buddhists began with an idea but no funds to create the café they envisaged, so they reached out to the Sheffield Buddhist Centre and found such enthusiasm from its members that loans and donations soon made the venture possible. Its name means 'generosity' in Sanskrit – a heartfelt thank you to everyone who contributed time, money and skills to the project – and its ethos is based on a set of core values shared by everyone in the team.

Decision-making is made collectively in a process that also looks after the wellbeing of everyone involved with the café. "We really value communication," explains Amalasiddhi, "and aim to have a really positive working environment with clear values that we all commit to." These include not harming other living beings but instead benefitting them and each other, and displaying the generosity that gave the café its start. They aim to give back, not just to those who supported Dana's establishment, but to the Buddhist centre and local charities through donations from the café's profits.

Amalasiddhi, the café's main chef, is already in the process of developing a more plant-based menu, using fruit and vegetables from their local grocery and wholesale supplier Lembas for quality vegan ingredients. "Our beliefs spill over into our interactions here – not to preach at all, but just to make everyone feel very welcome – so this really becomes a community space where even we are surprised by the wonderful mixture of customers, including our many regulars, who visit Dana and support us."

DANA
MEXICAN BREAKFAST

On this plate, I've brought together the flavours I love the most from my native Mexico. The recipe that follows is written down as my mother would have made it. For the salsa, you can use the chillies of your choice and add more or less depending on your heat tolerance.

250g quinoa
I pack of tortillas

For the black bean stew:
I tbsp vegetable oil
½ onion, finely sliced
2 cloves of garlic, finely chopped
250g tinned black beans
5g salt

For the spicy tomato scrambled tofu:
I tbsp vegetable oil
½ onion, finely sliced
2 cloves of garlic, finely chopped
½ tsp chilli flakes
6 tomatoes, roughly chopped
250g firm tofu
½ tsp salt

For the guacamole:
2 ripe avocadoes
I clove of garlic, finely chopped
I fresh lemon, juiced
½ tsp salt

For the salsa:
4 red chillies
3 tomatoes
¼ white onion
I clove of garlic
½ tsp salt

Put the quinoa and 500ml of water into a pan and cook on a medium heat for 25 minutes or until the quinoa has absorbed all the water and is lovely and fluffy.

For the black bean stew

In a separate pan, cook the onions in the oil for 5 minutes on a medium heat or until they turn light brown, then add the garlic and cook for a further 2 minutes. Add the black beans and salt then cook on a low heat for 10 minutes.

For the spicy tomato scrambled tofu

In another pan, cook the onions in the oil for 5 minutes on a medium heat or until they turn light brown, then add the garlic and the chilli flakes and cook for a further 2 minutes. Add the chopped tomatoes and cook for 5 minutes on a medium heat. Crush the tofu by hand or with a fork to create a 'scrambled' effect, then add to the pan with the salt. Cook for 10 minutes.

For the guacamole

Scoop the flesh out of the avocados and transfer it to a bowl. Add the rest of the ingredients and mash them with a fork or purée with a hand blender. It is more traditional to have your guacamole quite textured rather than a smooth paste.

For the salsa

Remove the stems from the chillies, and place the tomatoes and chillies in a pan. Add water until the tomatoes are covered. Cook for 10 minutes. Drain the water. Place the tomatoes, chillies, onion and garlic into a blender (or into a bowl if using a hand blender) and blend until smooth. Add the salt.

To serve

Warm the tortillas in the oven at 200°c for I minute and then plate everything together.

WORD ON
THE STREET

*Deckards have brought out a vegan menu to celebrate veggies in full force
and bring you vibrant flavours from around the globe, street food style.*

Deckards is the brainchild of co-owners Dec and Nico, who launched their venture in early 2017 at Bustler in Derby – one of the area's biggest food markets – and have since had two residencies, done private catering, popped up at many more public events and built up a following, thanks to their uniquely vibrant and accessible food offering. Deckards can now be found at Barrow Boy amidst the evolving foodie scene on Sheffield's Abbeydale Road.

The pair originally began with bao, not a regular feature on UK menus at that time, and moved on to burgers and other hands-on epicurean delights. With their roots firmly in the street food scene, Dec and Nico brought their brand to the attention of vegans with the addition of Tuesday veggie nights, launched in early 2019. Celebrating the humble but beautiful vegetable and following the same format as their regular menu, this dedicated weekly event was introduced as a more ethical direction for the business and has garnered great responses from the local community so far.

Their food's pan-Asian influences mingle with references to pop culture, though nothing is ruled out when it comes to flavour; cuisines from around the globe are drawn on when inspiration strikes and a new dish is developed. Pho with silken tofu, aubergine katsu curry, loaded fries…mixing comfort with the unknown is the kitchen's forte, and dishes are presented in a vibrant and approachable way that lets great ingredients speak for themselves.

The casual dining experience is as laid-back as its creators, who still run the whole venture between them, with the invaluable help of their Sheffield-based staff member, Harry. Deckards has a residency at Barrow Boy which means that the boys can serve up great grub six days a week from the kitchen there. The cosy venue is open Monday through Saturday with vegetarian options always available.

A generous helping of support from friends and family made Deckards possible, and its reach has since grown exponentially, gaining popularity and a nomination for the Street Food Exposed Awards 2019 along the way thanks to the wide appeal and top notch quality of the creative dishes they continue to roll out. In the words of Dec and Nico, "as long as it tastes good and looks good, we're happy!"

Photography: Jack Hague & Joshua Evers

DECKARDS
BBQ JERKED JACKFRUIT SANDO

We first discovered jackfruit on a trip overseas and fell in love with how versatile this product is; we knew from then it would be the go-to option for our veggie dishes. This stuff isn't hard to find either; you can pick some up at most Asian supermarkets. This recipe is ideal for family barbecues, dinner parties or any day of the week really!

For the jerk BBQ sauce:
3 cloves of garlic
15g ginger
1 Spanish onion
2 spring onions
2 tbsp olive oil
1 tbsp jerk seasoning
4 tbsp ketchup
4 tbsp mustard
1 tbsp molasses
200ml pineapple juice

For the jackfruit:
2 tins of young green jackfruit in water or brine
2 tbsp jerk seasoning
4 tbsp olive oil

For the pineapple salsa:
15g pineapple chunks
2 red peppers
1 red onion
15g fresh coriander
1 lime, juiced

For the red cabbage slaw:
1 red cabbage
1 red onion
2 limes, juiced

To serve:
1 burger bun of your choice
1 baby gem lettuce
1 tsp crispy onions

For the jerk BBQ sauce

Peel and finely chop the garlic, ginger, onion and spring onions. Heat a heavy-based pan on a medium heat and add the olive oil. Sweat the chopped ingredients for 5 minutes then add the jerk seasoning to the pan, mix and cook for a further 3 minutes. Add the ketchup, mustard, molasses and pineapple juice, stir everything together and simmer for 5 minutes.

For the jackfruit

Rinse, drain and thoroughly dry the jackfruit. Cover the jackfruit in jerk seasoning then set aside. Heat a large skillet over a medium heat then add 1 or two tablespoons of oil and the seasoned jackfruit to the pan. Cook for 2 to 3 minutes to add colour. Add the barbecue sauce, cook on a medium heat for 20 minutes and cover. Stir occasionally, ensuring the jackfruit doesn't stick to the base of the pan. Use two forks to shred the jackfruit as it cooks down to get a pulled texture. While this is simmering, make the salsa and slaw to accompany the dish.

Once the jackfruit has been properly simmered, increase the heat to medium-high and cook for a further 2 to 3 minutes, this will add extra colour and texture. This mixture can now be stored for up to 3 or 4 days in the fridge if you're not using it straightaway.

For the pineapple salsa

Finely dice the pineapple, peppers and red onion. Finely chop the coriander, removing the stalks. Mix everything together in a bowl, including the lime juice, and pop it in the fridge until serving.

For the red cabbage slaw

Finely slice the red cabbage, remembering to remove the core, and the red onion. We recommend using a mandolin to get a really fine slaw. Place the sliced onion and cabbage in a bowl then add the lime juice and season to taste with salt and pepper. Pop the slaw in the fridge until serving.

To serve

Slice the bun in half, place some gem lettuce on the bottom, add a generous amount of slaw, pile high with the BBQ jerked jackfruit and top it off with the pineapple salsa. Finally, sprinkle over some crispy onions for a bit of crunch, put the bun lid on and enjoy!

Preparation time: 10 minutes | Cooking time: 30 minutes | Serves: 4-6

HATCHING
A PLAN

In a former nineties club, one ambitious group of family and friends have created somewhere to satisfy your cravings and discover the heights of plant-based food, and they want to take it national…

Down The Hatch is a kitchen and cocktail bar determined to fill your belly with damn good food. The Liverpool venture has a pretty unique set up, from the underground location to the close-knit team. Jay and Conrad came up with the concept; they are co-owners and brothers-in-law who had an idea and ran with it. Their first business has proved so successful that they can't wait to push the same model across the North West and take their concept everywhere there's room for expansion.

Conrad's experience in the industry and Jay's education at "the best bar in Melbourne" formed the basis of their endeavours, along with a dedicated crew. Jay met his friend and flatmate Emily in Australia, who now does Hatch's marketing, and Rikki is the general manager but also Jay's sister, while barman Eli is Conrad's cousin. So when they say family run at Down The Hatch, they really mean it! The team is completed by head chef Tim Leah, who developed 2019's new menu.

DTH is almost totally vegan and includes quite a few gluten-free options, but puts the focus solely on good food no matter what your diet. "Our food is filling, satisfying, not particularly healthy… but honestly just the best you can get, in our opinion!" Burgers make up a chunk of the options, alongside deep fried indulgences and loaded fries to get your mouth watering. Everything is freshly cooked in-house, with the exception of buns and a few sauces, even down to the seitan which the kitchen team make daily to their own recipe.

It's all about innovating, evolving, looking ahead and enacting simple changes to create food for everyone at Down The Hatch. The cocktail bar serves an entirely vegan range of fruity, colourful drinks to enhance the food rather than overpower it, and by the same token there's always a bouncy, vibrant atmosphere but it's also important that guests feel at home. Jay describes the space as "raw and beautiful but also warm and cosy" and is proud of the unusual qualities that make the place special. The basement venue inspired its own name, which also hints at the owners' infectious enthusiasm for stuffing your face with irresistible junk food, no judgements allowed!

DOWN THE HATCH
INNER CITY SUMO

This recipe came about when Tim – DTH's head chef and a vegan himself – found himself slightly hungover and craving his favourite Chinese foods. Tofu, salt and pepper vegetables, 'prawn' crackers, crispy kale, soy sauce…it all went into a bun and the rest goes down in burger history!

For the marinade:
5ml white wine vinegar
150ml light soy sauce
½ tsp each of chilli flakes and five spice

For the filling:
Vegetable oil, for frying
200g firm tofu
1 large leaf of kale
1 sheet of rice paper
Pinch of chip spice*
2-3 tbsp coconut oil
½ a red and a green pepper, diced
1 spring onion, diced
1 small red chilli, diced

For the seasoning:
½ tsp five spice
½ tsp light brown sugar
¼ tsp ground ginger
1 tsp garlic paste
1 tsp salt
Pinch of chilli flakes

To build the burger:
1 burger bun, split in half
Dollop of vegan mayonnaise
1 large leaf of gem lettuce
1 thick slice of beef tomato

Using a whisk, combine all the ingredients for the marinade with 50ml of water. Transfer to a shallow tray or roasting dish. Slice the tofu into two rectangular steaks, about 5cm down the long side. Submerge these in the marinade and leave to absorb the flavours for 30 minutes.

Turn on a deep fat fryer, or fill half a large deep-sided saucepan with vegetable oil and heat. Drop the kale leaf in and deep fry for 10 seconds or until crispy. Remove with tongs and place onto kitchen towel to absorb excess oil.

Drop the sheet of rice paper into the oil and fry just until it puffs up into a 'cracker' – this only takes 2 or 3 seconds – then remove, place onto kitchen towel and dust both sides with chip spice. (*We use our own blend, but similar chip spices include paprika, onion powder, garlic powder, black pepper and salt so you could use a different brand or a mixture of these instead).

Heat a tablespoon of the coconut oil in a wok or frying pan, then add all of the veg seasoning. Fry for 5 to 10 seconds, making sure not to burn the spices. Add all the diced veg and fry until it softens, then set aside.

After marinating the tofu, shallow fry the steaks in coconut oil for 2 minutes on either side, or until crispy then place on kitchen roll.

To build the burger

Toast both sides of burger bun and spread some vegan mayonnaise on both surfaces. Lay the gem lettuce leaf on the bottom half, followed by the slice of beef tomato, the tofu steaks, sautéed veg, crispy kale leaf and rice cracker. Top with the bun lid and get it down the hatch!

Preparation time: 15 minutes, plus 30 minutes marinating | Cooking time: 15 minutes | Serves: 2

EIGHT DAYS
A WEEK

Eighth Day has been going for nearly half a century, providing Manchester with vegan and vegetarian food that puts the emphasis on health and wellbeing for both staff and customers.

As one of the first vegetarian establishments in Manchester, Eighth Day has built up a reputation for creative food and first-hand knowledge on taking care of yourself and the planet. The longstanding worker's co-operative has been on the same site since the early seventies. The current building was renovated in 2018 but retains the business' distinctive original 70s logo and its mission, albeit both slightly updated since then! The business was initially an alternative shop but has always stayed away from the traditional model of ownership, in order to really take care of the people who invest their time there.

Today, Eighth Day comprises a large café and shop that are both vegan and vegetarian, with an emphasis on health, wellbeing and ethical trading. This approach is reflected across the range and type of products stocked, the daily menu served and the team that own and manage this democratically run business. There is a wealth of diverse and specialised knowledge held within the workforce who make Eighth Day a destination for people interested in sports nutrition, cruelty-free beauty, professional dietary advice and much more, providing customers with a great reference point for plant-based lifestyles.

The café doesn't follow a set menu; the seven chefs create dishes following regular meetings, make collective decisions and work creatively on their initiative. "We have a lot of autonomy," says Stan, who is both a chef and the company secretary, "which means that our food is always exciting and also uses ingredients in a far less wasteful way, since we can cook with whatever is fresh that morning." Several times a year, the café transforms into an evening restaurant, serving three course dinners paired with cocktails and a refined, intricate approach to food. Other regular events include chocolate tasting, wine nights, and Sunday lunches for special occasions.

The café is fully licensed and serves a range of vegan alcoholic drinks – which are often improved with a dash of Eighth Day's homemade infusions and syrups – alongside fresh juices and smoothies so there's something for everyone. Eighth Day always looks to work with local businesses like Ancoats Coffee Co, who not only provide their packaging-free speciality coffee, but also train the café's baristas at their roastery in Manchester. From source to serving, Eighth Day is always building close relationships with suppliers, co-op members, and of course customers both time-honoured and new.

THE 8TH DAY

THE EIGHTH DAY
VEGAN·VEGETARIAN·SHOP·CAFE

GRIDDLED POLENTA STACK WITH BEET KETCHUP & PUMPKIN SEED ROCKET PESTO

This is a light dish which is great as a starter or a main course. The beet ketchup and rocket pesto are both longstanding Eighth Day recipes which we regularly serve in the café as side dishes for some of our main meals. They lend their flavours beautifully to the griddled polenta. The idea to serve all three together first came about during preparation for our Mediterranean-themed supper club in the spring of 2018.

For the beet ketchup:

2 tbsp sunflower or rapeseed oil

1 white onion

1 large beetroot

2 cloves of garlic

1 small knob of fresh ginger

1 400g tin of chopped tomatoes

2 tbsp cider vinegar

1 tbsp agave nectar or maple syrup

Pinch of cayenne pepper

Salt and pepper, to taste

For the pumpkin seed rocket pesto:

100g pumpkin seeds

100g rocket leaves

50g basil leaves

50g fresh parsley

1 lemon, juiced

150ml extra-virgin olive oil

For the polenta:

2 tbsp olive oil

2 cloves of garlic, crushed

A few fresh rosemary leaves

150g polenta

600ml vegetable stock

Salt and pepper, to taste

For the beet ketchup

Heat up the oil in a saucepan while you peel and dice the onion, then add it to the pan and stir to coat in oil. Sauté the onion for a couple of minutes. In the meantime, peel and dice the beetroot and garlic. Thoroughly wash the ginger then either grate or finely chop it. Add the prepared beetroot, garlic and ginger to the pan and stir to cover everything in oil. Cook for a few minutes on a moderate heat while stirring. Add the tin of tomatoes along with the vinegar, agave nectar and cayenne pepper. Bring everything to the boil then reduce the heat and place a lid on the pan. Simmer until all the vegetables are tender, which will take around 30 to 40 minutes. Season the ketchup to taste with salt and pepper, then blend to a smooth consistency using a stick blender.

For the pumpkin seed rocket pesto

Spread the pumpkin seeds out evenly on a baking tray and place into a preheated oven at 160°c for 5 minutes or until lightly toasted. Remove and allow to cool. Roughly chop all the leaves, then place all of the ingredients into a food processor and blitz until smooth. Season to taste with salt.

For the polenta

Heat up the oil in a deep saucepan, then add the garlic and rosemary. Cook while stirring for about 2 minutes. Add the polenta, stock and desired amount of seasoning before bringing to the boil. Simmer for 3 to 6 minutes while stirring until the polenta thickens.

Line a medium-size flat roasting dish with baking parchment and tip the cooked polenta onto it. Leave to cool at room temperature for 1 hour, then place in the fridge to set and leave for a minimum of 2 hours, or 4 if possible.

Once the polenta has set, check that it is firm prior to cutting (the pieces shouldn't fall apart and/or stick to the knife) then cut into evenly shaped rectangular pieces about 2cm thick. Flash fry each piece in a hot and oiled griddle pan over a high heat until the desired level of charring has been achieved. Remove from the pan using tongs and place on paper towels to absorb any excess oil.

To serve

Serve the griddled polenta over the beet ketchup as pictured and top with a few teaspoons of rocket pesto. Enjoy!

THE EIGHTH DAY
PUMPKIN CAKE AND COCONUT SORBET

A sweet, sticky, warmly spiced cake with a satisfyingly spongey texture. The recipe was originally dreamt up by one of our chefs for a Christmas treat and then perfected by another of our chefs (as is often the way with favourite Eighth Day recipes!). You will need an ice cream machine to make the sorbet, and a stick blender or food processor for the cake.

For the pumpkin purée:
500g cubed pumpkin or squash
150g sugar

For the pumpkin cake:
225g plain flour
225g dark muscovado sugar
50g caster sugar
3 tsp cinnamon
3 tsp ground ginger
1 tsp bicarbonate of soda
Pinch of salt
250g pumpkin purée
125ml sunflower oil
1 tsp vanilla essence
75g coconut milk
75g dried apricot, chopped

For the coconut sorbet:
250g sugar
200ml water
400g coconut milk
25ml white rum

For the pumpkin purée
Cook the pumpkin in simmering water until soft, then strain. Blend the cooked pumpkin or squash with the sugar to form a purée and set aside.

For the pumpkin cake
Preheat the oven to 160°c. Mix the flour, sugars, spices, bicarbonate of soda and salt together in a large bowl. Gradually add the pumpkin purée (leaving two tablespoons for garnish when serving) to the dry ingredients along with the sunflower oil, vanilla essence and coconut milk and then stir in the chopped apricot. Spoon the mixture into a loaf tin lined with greaseproof paper. Bake in the preheated oven for 50 minutes to 1 hour. Check that a knife comes out clean before removing from the oven. The cake should cool completely before being removed from the tin.

For the coconut sorbet
Heat the sugar and water to a simmer while whisking, then remove from the heat. Once off the heat, mix in the coconut milk and rum. Cool and then freeze in an ice cream machine.

Preparation time: 30 minutes | Cooking time: 1 hour | Serves: 4-6

GUILT-FREE
INDULGENCE

Eat well, live fit, treat often is the motto and the essence of Elly Joy, a sweet treat brand producing gluten-free and vegan products, including the incredibly popular Froconut®, in Sheffield.

Elly Blackwell set up her venture to bring gluten-free and vegan indulgence to more people who, like her, were on a quest for healthier sweet treats. The young entrepreneur is Sheffield-based and began by experimenting with bakes and snacks in her own kitchen, blogging and enjoying food photography. Over the course of a year and a half, she built up the business – eponymously and aptly named Elly Joy – by attending food festivals and markets, then upgraded to a refitted vintage horsebox which enabled her to cater for events such as weddings all over the UK.

Today, her business is thriving with a permanent residence at Cutlery Works in Kelham Island – Sheffield's indoor bar and food court, brand new as of November 2018 – and plenty of new developments on the horizon. Her entire range is gluten-free and plant-based and many are recreations of classic favourites, such as the Doughnots, stocked by Steam Yard and other quality cafés and coffee houses around Sheffield. The treats satisfy cravings as well as providing nutritional value; as the recipes steer clear of refined and processed ingredients, and instead use natural sugars to keep the flavours irresistible.

Colourful glazes, tempting toppings, and fun presentation make the treats appealing to anyone so that "you eat them first and then find out what's in them later" as Elly puts it! Her dairy-free ice cream alternative Froconut® is hugely popular both in her home town and on the road, served in halved coconut shells and sprinkled or decorated with all manner of imaginative and tempting sweets. A successful bid for SIP (Sheffield Innovation Programme) funding means that fans can expect the launch of Froconut® as a purchasable product to enjoy at home in the near future.

Elly still takes her passion for healthier living and eating to the people through event catering, and has enjoyed the scope of a wider menu at her Cutlery Works premises. "It offers more potential," she says, "so I'm excited to make more products available and am always looking for the next way to grow and expand – I'd love to have a second venue, for example, so more people can enjoy indulging guilt-free and discover dessert alternatives that are both fun, delicious and healthy."

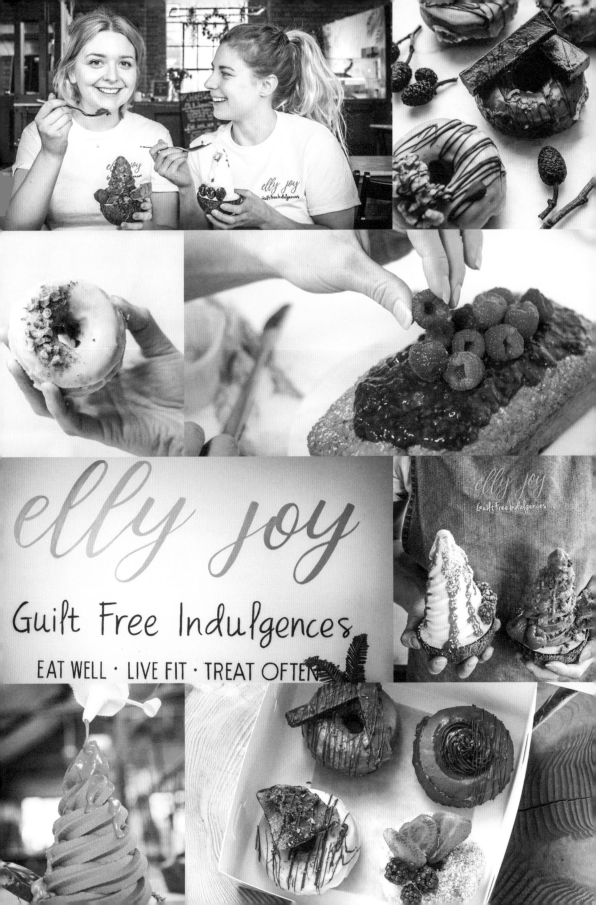

elly joy

Guilt Free Indulgences

EAT WELL · LIVE FIT · TREAT OFTEN

RASPBERRY AND COCONUT BANANA BREAD

This quick bake is perfect toasted then served with yoghurt and fruit as a healthy breakfast, or packed in your lunch box for a daily energising snack. Ideal for using up those uneaten bananas that are just starting to brown.

3 ripe bananas
90g oat flour
60g gluten-free self-raising flour
55g vegetable oil
55g agave nectar
125g raspberries
50g desiccated coconut

Preheat the oven to 150°c and line a loaf tin with non-stick baking parchment. Place all the ingredients, except the raspberries and coconut, into a mixing bowl. Beat by hand with a wooden spoon, or with an electric mixer, until everything is combined. Fold in the raspberries and coconut then transfer the mixture into the prepared tin.

Bake in the preheated oven for 40 to 60 minutes. When done, remove from the tin and place on a cooling rack before slicing and serving. This is best made the night before and enjoyed the morning after!

Preparation time: 10 minutes | Cooking time: 40-60 minutes | Serves: 10-12

FROCONUT®
PEANUT BUTTER AND HONEYCOMB FUDGE

This fudge is a perfect topping for Froconut® and such a simple treat to make at home.

400g dark chocolate

200g coconut cream (place a tin of full-fat coconut milk in the fridge overnight and use the solidified top part)

260g smooth peanut butter

200g vegan honeycomb

Melt the chocolate and coconut cream in a saucepan over a low heat until combined and smooth. Remove from heat and stir in peanut butter until fully mixed in. Add chunks of honeycomb into the mixture, reserving some for the top.

Pour the fudge mixture into a lined baking tin, sprinkle over the remaining honeycomb and place in the fridge for at least 90 minutes. Once set, remove from the fridge and leave for 10 minutes at room temperature before cutting into squares. Enjoy with Froconut® or as a treat on its own!

Preparation time: 5 minutes, plus 90 minutes setting | Cooking time: 5 minutes | Serves: 15

PURE, NATURAL,
WHOLESOME

Filmore and Union is on a mission to make people feel good by offering pure, natural, wholesome and satisfying food and drink with a 'neighbourhood dining' vibe in more than 16 locations across the North.

Filmore and Union was founded in 2011 by entrepreneur and mum of three, Adele Ashley. She was frustrated by the lack of healthy restaurant and take-out options for someone who knew first hand why eating pure, natural, wholesome food was so important in changing the way you feel. A trip to San Francisco – the land of healthy eating and great service – inspired the new venture's name courtesy of her two favourite streets in the sunny Californian city. In 2012, the first Filmore and Union restaurant was opened in the centre of York.

The business grew up around Adele's vision of becoming a household name known for making people feel good. "We want to be more than a chain of restaurants; we want to be a wellness and lifestyle brand, a go-to place for inspiration, advice and support amongst like-minded people."

Now you can find Filmore and Union restaurants, take-outs and even concessions in John Lewis across York, Newcastle, Leeds and Harrogate, serving breakfast, lunch and Sunday brunches with an extensive vegan menu. Each location has a unique feel – Adele only likes buildings with character, such as the former York minster choir school that now houses one of her restaurants – but is linked to the brand's strong ethos by the food and drink served. Pure, natural and wholesome are words to live by for the staff, who are passionate about bringing innovative and convenient options to people from all walks of life, including their dogs for most venues!

The kitchens make almost everything on-site, and the company has its own gluten-free bakery, where vegan bread and plenty of delicious cakes are created to be enjoyed alongside a cup of Filmore and Union's own organic coffee blend. Many of the venues stay open into the evening and all offer customisable dishes to suit individual tastes and dietary requirements. Fresh juices, made with nothing but locally supplied fruit and veg, are a big part of the daytime menu as well as breakfast and brunch items you can eat any time of day.

The feeling of a relaxed, community hub born out of the desire to make people happy through food and drink characterises each Filmore and Union location, so those in search of wellness, health, happiness and very tasty treats should look no further than their nearest!

ROASTED TOFU AND SWEET POTATO RENDANG CURRY

A firm favourite at all our vegan supper clubs. You will struggle not to eat this as you go along but believe us, it is so worth the wait! Enjoy as your kitchen fills with delicious scents of exotic spices.

3 tsp oil of your choice

180g sweet potato

225g firm tofu, drained and 2cm cubed

60g pak choi

45g edamame beans

For the rendang curry sauce:

1 small white onion, diced

2cm piece of fresh ginger, grated

3 cloves of garlic, crushed

1 lemongrass stalk, finely chopped

1 tsp each of ground cumin, cinnamon, nutmeg and coriander

1 tbsp turmeric

20g muscovado sugar

15g each of tamari and tamarind paste

½ tsp chilli flakes (add extra if you like a kick!)

400g tin of coconut milk

For the coconut rice:

150g brown rice

65g black rice

25g desiccated coconut

400g tin of coconut milk

To garnish (optional):

Small bunch of fresh coriander

Sliced chillies

Crushed peanuts

Lime juice

Preheat the oven to 200°c. Peel and cube the sweet potato, toss in a teaspoon of the oil and add to a baking tray. Cook for 30 minutes until tender. In the meantime you can start your rendang curry sauce which should take about 15 minutes.

For the rendang curry sauce

Add the remaining two teaspoons of oil to a wok and place on a medium heat. Add the onion, ginger, garlic and lemongrass. Fry for 5 minutes until the ingredients have softened. Add the ground spices, muscovado sugar, tamari, tamarind paste, dried chilli flakes and the tin of coconut milk. Turn the heat down and simmer. After 15 minutes, take the pan off the heat and let the sauce cool.

Check on the sweet potato cubes and turn them to prevent sticking. Drain the tofu, slice into 2cm cubes and then place these on a baking tray lined with greaseproof paper. Place in the oven for the remaining 15 minutes.

For the coconut rice

Place a medium-sized saucepan on a medium heat. Place the brown rice, black rice, desiccated coconut and coconut milk into the pan. Gradually add 300ml of water until the rice is soft and all liquid has cooked out. Season with a sprinkling of salt if you wish.

Remove the tofu and sweet potatoes from the oven. They should be lovely and roasted by now! The curry sauce should have cooled a little, so blend using a stick blender until it is nice and smooth. Once you have done this, you're ready to start plating up.

Reheat the curry sauce on a medium heat and add the pak choi, edamame beans, sweet potato and tofu. Stir until heated through. Reheat the coconut rice if needed by placing it in a small bowl and place this in the microwave for no longer than 1 minute.

To plate

Spoon some rice into a bowl and pour the curry around it. To add a little extra flavour, why not garnish with some freshly picked coriander, sliced chilli, crushed peanuts and a squeeze of lime juice? Delicious!

Preparation time: 15 minutes | Cooking time: approx. 1 hour | Serves 3

IT'S EASY
BEING GREEN

Fate, or something like it, stepped in when two Simons
with a shared vision accidentally opened a restaurant…

Greens was established in 1990 and has stood the test of time, evolving as the food scene changed around it and embracing the move from a vegetarian restaurant to one with a mostly vegan menu. Simon Connolly and Simon Rimmer quickly became friends while working at a restaurant in Didsbury, joking that they could run a business should the opportunity arise. When it did, they realised that each was serious about food and wanted to give their own restaurant a proper go, despite not having any experience in the kitchen but knowing front of house was their strength.

The pair chanced on the perfect venue, and discussed hypothetical plans over a beer and curry that evening, not knowing that the very next morning a 'For Sale' sign would go up outside the café they'd earmarked, just as Simon happened to be driving past! The new owners began developing a menu; they weren't vegetarian themselves but were excited about the beginnings of a new wave of cuisine, and wanted to challenge preconceived ideas about vegetarian meals. Within a short space of time, Greens became known for luxuriously indulgent food – especially opulent desserts – but wasn't initially favoured by vegans as dairy was then a mainstay of the menu.

However, Simon and Simon saw veganism coming before it really took off in the UK and reacted accordingly. They expanded their knowledge of plant-based eating and went from a few vegan dishes to around three quarters of the menu being vegan-friendly. This change felt organic for the restaurant and helped to lighten its menu, even introducing the kitchen to great new suppliers. Ice Shack – just around the corner – became Greens' sole ice cream provider thanks to its fantastic vegan flavours, and the craft beers are all vegan and locally sourced.

These shifts in direction have never been about preaching to the customer, but simply about giving "the best food and the best service we can provide," Simon explains. "We always try to be inclusive and the main goal is for people to have fun. Our staff make the experience positive, without revering the food and being stuffy about dining out." Ever forward-thinking, the business partners are now working on a collaboration with a venue that will allow them to cater for weddings and private parties with Greens' food and staff, taking the ethos and much-loved food to more people than ever.

SOBA NOODLE SALAD, SMOKED TOFU, KOREAN BARBECUE DRESSING

This is a very simple recipe with relatively few ingredients that produces a dish that packs a real flavour hit but is perfectly balanced.

For the dressing:

25g garlic, chopped

50g fresh ginger, chopped

1 fresh red chilli, chopped

100ml light soy sauce

30g maple syrup

100ml rice wine vinegar

50ml sesame oil

1 tsp sesame seeds, toasted

100g dark brown sugar

1 tsp Korean red chilli paste

For the salad:

500g soba noodles

200g smoked tofu

Oil, for deep frying

24 stalks of tenderstem broccoli

180g edamame beans, shelled

180g peanuts

3 red peppers

1 tbsp sesame seeds

3 fresh limes

12 sprigs of coriander

For the dressing

The dressing needs to be made in advance to allow time for the it to cool. This recipe will make more than you need to serve six, but will keep in the refrigerator in a sealed container for a week. Place all the ingredients except the Korean chilli paste in a pan and gently bring to the boil. Add the Korean chilli paste then simmer for 20 minutes. Blend the dressing with a stick blender and pass through a sieve. Allow to cool.

For the salad

Start by cooking the soba noodles as per instructions on the packet, cool under running water and drain. Next, cube the smoked tofu into 1cm pieces and deep fry at 180°c for 2 minutes until crispy, then set aside to drain. Then grill the broccoli stalks on a chargrill for 5 minutes, turning once. Cook the edamame beans in the microwave; cover with water in a microwaveable dish and cook for 4 minutes. You can use frozen cooked edamame if you wish. Roast the peanuts for 5 minutes at 180°c and toast the sesame seeds at the same time. Finally, slice the peppers into thin strips.

Now combine all the salad ingredients except the limes, sesame seeds and coriander in a large mixing bowl and add enough dressing to coat them.

To serve

Divide the salad between six plates or shallow bowls. Top each dish with half a lime, two sprigs of coriander and a sprinkle of sesame seeds.

STRONG AND
NORTHERN

Henderson's Relish is a Sheffield institution that is both a closely guarded secret and the city's pride and joy. And this spicy Yorkshire sauce is perfect for vegans, too!

The story of Henderson's Relish began in 1885, in the general store of a man named Henry Henderson. This pioneer first sold his creation from large wooden barrels that filled customers' glass bottles with a 'strong and northern' sauce unlike any other. Henderson's grew in popularity and in 1910 production moved to the now iconic factory on Leavygreave Road, Sheffield.

Loved by Sheffielders for generations, today the unique taste of Henderson's Relish is being discovered by vegans nationwide. It doesn't use animal products and is free from gluten. The exact recipe is known only to three family members, who still own the business and make the secret mix for every batch.

Whether you splash it on pie, stew, chips, 'cheese' on toast or add a finishing touch to a homemade burger, Henderson's Relish completes any dish. It's also used by chefs as an ingredient; it is free from allergens and is low in salt, so is suitable for all diets and meals.

"Once you've tried Henderson's Relish, you're hooked. It has a wonderful, unique spicy taste – a strong and northern family favourite!" says Matt Davies, general manager of Henderson's. "Henderson's Relish is Sheffield; unassuming, welcoming and proudly independent."

Recently, it's become easier to enjoy Henderson's Relish across the north of England, as it's available in grocery stores and major supermarkets regionally. It can also be ordered online through the company website.

The newly-launched miniature bottle has been a popular addition. Starting life as 'Holiday Hendo's' – for Sheffielders to take away where their special sauce couldn't be found – the 31ml glass bottles are now an essential travel accessory and wedding favour for vegan and Sheffield celebrations; a happy marriage of everything most loved!

TOMATO AND WILD GARLIC PESTO TART WITH HENDERSON'S RELISH ONIONS

PJ Taste are champions of seasonally inspired local food, delivering delicious and creative catering for business events and family celebrations all over Sheffield and Derbyshire. As well as being famous for our Sheffield Egg, we are proud to be developing our own forest garden. This supplies a range of sustainably grown fruit, edible flowers, herbs and salads, as well as more unusual perennial vegetables. Our plot also has wild areas for foraging and plenty of space for our bees. This produce helps inform our menus and is the inspiration for a wealth of vegan dishes, including this flavoursome tart which doubles up as an impressive dinner party starter or rustic lunch.

For the wild garlic pesto:
65g pumpkin seeds
100g wild garlic leaves
1 lemon, zested and juiced
Salt and pepper
120ml olive oil

For the Henderson's Relish caramelised onions:
4 white onions, sliced
Splash of olive oil
Henderson's Relish

For the tomato tart:
6 ripe tomatoes (local and grown in season are ideal)
Henderson's Relish
Salt and pepper
Sprig of thyme
1-2 cloves of garlic, finely chopped
1 pack of ready-made vegan puff pastry
Soya milk (or other vegan milk)
Handful of pumpkin, sunflower and sesame seeds

For the wild garlic pesto

This is best made in March or April, but can give way to a fresh herb salsa made with parsley, dill mint, coriander or others later in the year. Using a food processor, blend the pumpkin seeds with the wild garlic (or mixed herbs), lemon zest and juice, salt, pepper and olive oil.

For the Henderson's Relish caramelised onions

Slowly sweat down the sliced onions in a pan with a little olive oil, adding Henderson's Relish and seasoning to taste. The onions will gradually darken until sticky, dark brown and unctuous.

For the tomato tart

Using beautiful multi-coloured heritage tomatoes (we buy these from Sheffield Organic Growers) in the summer makes for a real treat. Prepare the tomatoes by slicing them onto a baking tray lined with baking parchment. Season with Henderson's Relish, salt and pepper, thyme and garlic. Toss everything together then bake in an oven at 170°c for 45 minutes. This draws out some moisture and intensifies the flavour.

While the tomatoes are cooking, roll out the puff pastry to the size of an A4 sheet of paper and approximately 2mm thick. Score a 2cm border right around the outside and brush the whole sheet with soya milk. Add a thin base layer of caramelised onions within the border you have made. Next place the sliced tomatoes around the tart. Finally, sprinkled mixed seeds carefully around the border. Bake in the oven at 180°c for 30 to 40 minutes, checking to achieve a nicely browned pastry edge.

To serve

Let the tart cool slightly and serve with a dollop of pesto on top, offering bottles of Henderson's Relish for people to 'dress' their slice at the table. Great with new potatoes and seasonal salad for a rustic lunch.

Preparation time: 30 minutes | Cooking time: approx. 1 hour 40 minutes | Serves: 2

TOMATO ARANCINI WITH HENDERSON'S RELISH

We opened Pour because we love pizza and beer, and we felt the Heeley area of Sheffield was crying out for more vegan options. All our food and drink is vegan as standard, though vegetarian cheese is available by request. Everyone's welcome, especially if they bring their dog!
Arancini are deep-fried and stuffed risotto balls. They hail from Italy and take their name from the 'little oranges' which they resemble when the breadcrumb coating turns crisp and golden. The Henderson's Relish in our recipe adds a similar depth to the dish that balsamic vinegar does in Italy.

For the risotto:
50ml olive oil
½ onion, finely chopped
1 clove of garlic, finely chopped
100g Arborio rice
75ml white wine
500ml vegetable stock
25ml Henderson's Relish
250g tomato passata
½ tsp dried basil
½ tsp dried oregano
½ tsp salt
½ tsp sugar

For the filling:
50g vegan cheese, grated

For the coating:
50g flour
200ml soy milk (unsweetened)
50g breadcrumbs
Oil, for frying
Splash of Henderson's Relish

Fry the onions and garlic in olive oil on a low heat until softened, but don't allow them to colour. Add the rice and stir well to coat all the grains in the oil. Tip in the wine and turn up the heat until it's bubbling, then add the stock, the Henderson's Relish, the passata, the herbs, salt and sugar then reduce the heat to a low simmer. Stir frequently until all the liquid is absorbed and the risotto is creamy but the rice still has a slight firmness to it. You may need to add more stock to get it to the perfect consistency.

Remove from the heat and add seasoning to taste, then spread the risotto out on a baking tray and leave to cool completely, preferably in the fridge. When cool, take a tablespoonful of the risotto between your palms and form a ball a little larger than a golf ball. Make a hole in the middle and fill it with a marble-sized ball of grated cheese then reform the risotto around the filling, using extra to patch up if needed. Repeat until all the risotto is used up then chill again in the fridge.

Take three separate bowls and fill with the flour, soy milk and breadcrumbs. Roll each risotto ball first in flour, then in milk, then breadcrumbs until fully covered. Using one hand for dry ingredients and the other for wet will cut down on the messiness!

When all the balls are coated, fry them in batches in a deep fat fryer at 170°c until golden. Alternatively, shallow fry them in a pan making sure to turn regularly to ensure even cooking. Drain on kitchen towel and serve with a garnish of rocket, other salad leaves or a tomato salsa. Splash Henderson's Relish on top for the essential finishing touch!

Preparation time: 15 minutes, plus 30 minutes cooling | Cooking time: 30 minutes | Serves: 4

HENDERSON'S YORKSHIRE PUDDINGS & GRAVY

Wapentake is 'A Little Piece of Yorkshire' nestled on Kirkgate, one of the oldest streets in Leeds. It's parallel to Leeds Kirkgate Market that we so frequently use for ingredients. Our menu covers brunch to hearty classics with a vegan alternative for every option. We are all about supporting local and fresh produce sourced from our lovely Yorkshire doorstep. While working on our vegan alternatives we could not refrain from creating one of the county's most famed culinary creations! So here it is, to complete your Sunday dinner or enjoy as a snack.

For the gravy:
1 onion
2 carrots
1 head of celery
1 veggie stock cube
75ml Henderson's Relish (at least!)
2½lt water
50g cornflour

For the puddings:
325g plain flour
Pinch of salt and pepper
1 tbsp baking powder
600ml soya milk
25ml Henderson's Relish
A smidge of vegetable oil

For the gravy

Chop all the vegetables as chunky or skinny as you like, plonk them in a tall saucepan and begin to roast them off. Add the stock cube with a couple of lashings of Henderson's Relish and continue cooking until the vegetables are beginning to brown. Pour in the water and leave your concoction on a low-medium heat to reduce for about 1 hour (usually a good time to make a brew, it's thirsty work). After this time, sieve out the veg, add all the Henderson's Relish – if you can't get enough of the spicy sauce, we applaud adding more, fill ya boots – and the taste test comes in handy till you get it to your liking. Make a paste with the cornflour and a dab of water then whisk it in to the gravy. Then my dears, you are done!

For the Yorkshire puddings

Sieve the flour, salt, pepper and baking powder together in to a mixing bowl. Add the soya milk and Henderson's Relish while whisking everything together to create your batter. Cover the bowl – a tea towel will do – and leave the batter to stand in the fridge for 5 to 10 minutes. While the batter chills, pour a smidge of oil into each hole of your Yorkshire pudding tray then place it in the oven at 220°c to heat for 5 minutes. Evenly pour the batter into the tray and leave to cook for 10 to 15 minutes before rotating the tray and cooking for another 10 to 15 minutes for a lovely even finish.

To serve

Lather the gravy on top of your puds and splash some more Henderson's Relish over the top for good measure.

Preparation time: 15-20 minutes | Cooking time: 1 hour 45 minutes | Serves: 8-12 (with a mugful or two of gravy left over)

SUSHI, BUT NOT AS
YOU KNOW IT

York has embraced its new insight to the authentic flavours and contemporary inventions of Japan thanks to fabulous food and drink at Ippuku Tea House.

Ippuku Tea House was set up in 2017 by Frances Ozaki and her husband Tatsu, who wanted to bring something authentic to the locals in their city. The couple took over an existing café in York and refurbished the venue to create a haven of Japanese food, service and atmosphere that reflects the country's culinary scene today.

Being a tea house, Ippuku of course has an impressive selection of Japanese varieties from the enduringly popular sencha to the finest matcha. These are supplied by Tatsu's business, also called Ippuku, which he began before the couple started the tea house to offer real Japanese tea wholesale to London and further afield. Links with other London-based suppliers mean that Japanese food is also readily available for the café menu.

Many dishes are very recognisable to the average York resident, but it was important to Frances that Ippuku Tea House branched out to include contemporary and inventive options that represent Japan's prowess and enthusiasm when it comes to experimenting and modernising their food and drink. Most of her chefs are Japanese, with the rest of the team a mix between British and Japanese nationals like the founding couple. Some sourcing is also done by staff and Tatsu's family, so there's never a shortage of new products to try.

Seasonal specials make the most of winter or summer cravings, such as a hearty British-Japanese crossover beef and potato stew or one of Japan's most popular dishes, simmered miso mackerel. Small bites like yakitori and gyoza can be followed by vegetable curry or a sushi bowl, but there's plenty of opportunity to be more adventurous and try a 'sushi sandwich' – crispy rice layers where you'd normally find bread, encasing a filling of your choice – then perhaps a mochi (soft rice cake) ice cream for dessert!

About half of Ippuku's menu is vegan and everything made in the kitchen is gluten-free too. The tea house is open for lunch, afternoon treats and dinner with restaurant service and a license to serve a wonderful combination of original recipe cocktails made with Japanese spirits, whiskies, and sake alongside beers and wines.

Ippuku aims to welcome visitors and its many regulars with a down-to-earth and homely atmosphere, amidst cosy lantern-lit tables and sunny courtyard seats. The pretty venue hosts regular events too, so is a hotspot for language, culture, craft and many more hobbies or interests.

GINGER TOFU

We are big fans of tofu; almost all varieties feature on our menu throughout the year. But this way of preparing tofu is the house favourite. It is very versatile so you can use it in many different recipes. In Japanese, 'shouga' is ginger and 'yaki' is grill. The sauce is commonly eaten with pork in Japan, but we want everyone to enjoy it, so we made this vegan version and it hasn't left the menu since!

For the shougayaki sauce:

45ml soy sauce

50ml mirin

25ml cooking sake (white wine can be used instead)

12g sugar

20ml water

10g fresh ginger, finely grated

For the tofu:

200g firm tofu

200g onions

10g fresh ginger

4 tbsp potato starch

1 tbsp sesame oil

For the shougayaki sauce

Put all of the shougayaki sauce ingredients in a pan and heat until the sugar has dissolved, then remove from the heat. This sauce can also be used with many other ingredients and will store well in a sealed container in the fridge.

For the tofu

Remove the tofu from its packaging, and wrap the block in white paper towels. Place in a microwaveable dish and heat on a high setting for 2 minutes. If you don't have a microwave, put another heavy dish on top of the tofu block and weight it down carefully. The pressure will help remove the water; you can do this for at least 10 minutes, depending on the texture of tofu you want. When water has been removed, the tofu should still be moist but not soaking wet and you can remove the paper towels and drain off the water.

While the tofu is draining, cut the onions into 1cm thick slices end to end so that it holds together. Peel the fresh ginger and cut it into long thin slices. Now cut the prepared tofu block into roughly 2½ cm cubes. You should have about 12 pieces per person or 100g each. Put the tofu cubes into a large freezer bag, add the potato starch, seal the bag and gently shake the tofu around until covered with starch. This is the most effective method but similar results can be achieved by mixing together with your hands in a bowl.

To cook

Heat the sesame oil on a medium to high heat in a non-stick frying pan, then add the onions and tofu. Gently turn everything over in the pan with a spatula to evenly coat the tofu in the oil. Fry for a further 3 minutes, then add the ginger and shougayaki sauce to the frying pan. Keep moving everything around with the spatula so all the tofu, ginger and onion is evenly coated in the sauce. Keep on a medium to high heat until the sauce begins to simmer and thicken slightly.

To serve

This dish is nice served alongside a crunchy salad and sticky white rice. Be daring and put the tofu straight on top of either so the sauce covers everything!

Preparation time: 25 minutes | Cooking time: 10 minutes | Serves: 2

CHICKPEA TERIYAKI SKEWERS

This is one of our own inventions, as we wanted to find something tasty to have on a skewer for our vegan customers. This is our take on an izakaya (Japanese bar) dish, yakitori, inspired by a sticky summer treat called mitarashi dango. Both are grilled and glazed in a sweet and salty soy-based sauce, with a delightful soft texture, just like these teriyaki chickpea patties.

For the chickpea skewers:
400g tin of chickpeas
4 tbsp potato starch
½ tsp xanthan gum
3 tsp vegetable oil
Bunch of spring onions (about six)
12 x 10cm skewers

For the teriyaki sauce:
45ml soy sauce
50ml mirin
37½ml sake (1½ shots)
20g sugar

For the chickpea skewers

The best way to make these is with a food processor but similar results can be achieved mashing by hand. Drain the chickpeas and try to squeeze out as much liquid as possible. Put the drained chickpeas, potato starch, xantham gum and one teaspoon of the vegetable oil into a food processor. Blend until smooth. You may have to stop the mixer a few times and use a rubber spatula to scrape down the sides so everything is incorporated evenly.

Empty the mixture into a bowl and make sure the potato starch has been combined thoroughly. With clean hands pinch off a small amount of the mixture (we usually make 30g patties) and roll into a ball between your palms. Then gently press down into a patty shape and use your fingers to completely smooth out the edge and make sure there are no cracks. This will stop it from falling off the skewer. You should be able to make about 12 patties.

Put all of your patties on a tray or plate covered in baking parchment and put in the fridge to set. At this stage they will keep for up to 3 days in a sealed container. They should only take about 15 minutes to set, when the starch should absorb all the liquid from the chickpeas and make the patties firmer for easier frying.

For the teriyaki sauce

Put all the ingredients into a small pan and heat until the sugar has dissolved, and then remove from the heat. Cut the spring onions into 5cm batons. You need 12, enough for two per skewer, and the thicker white part of the onions is best for this.

To build the skewer

Lay the first patty on a board and push the skewer horizontally through the centre of it. Skewer a spring onion baton through the middle, then another patty and then another spring onion. Repeat for each skewer.

Heat up the remaining vegetable oil in a non-stick pan on a medium heat. Lay two skewers flat in the pan and fry on each side until golden brown. Use a fork to lift the end of the skewer and a spatula to flip it. Then add 50ml of the prepared teriyaki sauce to the pan and cook for a minute on each side on a high heat.

To serve

Place the grilled and glazed skewers in a small shallow dish and pour the remaining sauce over the top. Great for parties and indulgent snacking, especially accompanied by a beer!

Preparation time: 20 minutes | Cooking time: 5 minutes | Serves: 3

IPPUKU TEA HOUSE
YUZU CHOCOLATE CAKE

Yuzu is a Japanese citrus fruit with a lemony-orange flavour that's very popular in Japan and goes well with sweet and savoury dishes. You can find yuzu juice online or in large supermarkets. Our yuzu chocolate cake is a favourite among customers and staff; most people eat and enjoy it without even realising that it's vegan and gluten-free!

Dry ingredients:

275g Dove's self-raising flour

175g caster sugar

4 tbsp high quality raw cocoa powder

1 tsp xantham gum (gf)

1 tsp baking powder (gf)

¼ tsp baking soda (gf)

Wet ingredients:

150g vegan spread (we use Vitalite)

60g golden syrup

1 tbsp yuzu juice

300ml soya milk (or any other plant-based milk)

For the icing:

200g icing sugar

4 tbsp high quality raw cocoa powder

75g vegan spread

2 tbsp yuzu juice

For the cake

Preheat the oven to 180°c and prepare two 18cm round silicone cake moulds or parchment-lined cake tins. Sieve all of the dry ingredients into a large bowl and combine with a whisk.

In a microwaveable bowl or a small pan, melt 150g of the vegan spread and golden syrup until it just reaches liquid stage. Then pour this on top of the dry ingredients. Immediately add the soya milk and yuzu juice and mix all the wet and dry ingredients together until smooth and well combined.

Pour the batter evenly into the two cake moulds or lined tins, and then place them on the middle shelf of the preheated oven for 25 to 30 minutes (until a skewer comes out clean). Take out and leave to cool slightly in the moulds or tins on a cooling rack. When slightly cooler remove from the moulds or tins and leave to cool completely.

For the icing

Mix all the ingredients together and sandwich the cakes with half the icing. Cover the whole thing with the rest of the icing and decorate with liberty!

Chef's tips

We recommend using gluten-free flour as it will make the cake much lighter. Don't leave the mix out too long before putting the cake in the oven though, as gluten free flour absorbs more liquid than wheat flour and also the baking powder and soda will have been activated.

Preparation time: 20 minutes | Cooking time: 30 minutes | Serves: 8 (in Yorkshire slices)

LEAPS AND
BOUNDS

Mouth-watering plant-based takes on fast food is the name of the game at Jumping Bean, a comforting place, open for everyone, with a completely vegan menu and buzzing atmosphere.

Sara and Kayvan are siblings who were brought up in a vegan household – their grandparents first adopted the lifestyle during the Second World War – so they had years of family recipes under their belts when Kayvan decided to set up a healthy eating vegetarian cafe in 2012. With the advent of similar food and drink appearing in every supermarket though, it got harder to stay original, so in 2018 Sara reinvented Jumping Bean as a haven for vegan junk food. "We wanted to go completely vegan to protect the environment and to avoid any suffering or harm to animals as much as possible. The junk food idea came about as it was more niche, so there was definitely a gap in the market" says Sara.

Today Jumping Bean is run by Sara and Kayvan, with support from Sara's partner and dad. The aim is to provide a place not only for vegan and vegetarian diners, but also carnivores wanting to have their meat and eat it! This is made easy by the eatery offering burgers and hot dogs, with all kinds of irresistible toppings that offer delicious alternatives to meat, alongside naturally vegan creations. The menu is completed by a range of sweet shakes, hot drinks, cakes and brownies for ultimate indulgence. Everything is freshly made to order, using veg from the local greengrocer and supplies supporting other small businesses. Jumping Bean promises to have a 100% plant-based menu for everyone to enjoy, to use fresh locally sourced ingredients and organic where possible, and to use compostable packaging.

Since the move in this new direction, the plan is to keep spreading the vegan message and potentially expand to another venue in future. Jumping Bean has hit on something everyone loves now and then – a spot of naughtiness – but with the added bonus of ingredients that create much less impact on our environment and harm to animals. The daytime vibe is relaxed and open to all, encouraging locals to make it a regular hang out, and the later openings on Fridays and Saturdays provide an opportunity for events or an evening out with friends, family, even as a solo treat.

Ever the family affair, the business' name was thought up by Sara and Kayvan's mum to convey the kind of atmosphere they wanted to create, and refers to the great coffee served (OCC COFFEE) that's a perfect match for the American-style, but very much locally-grown, menu and inspiration at Jumping Bean.

JUMPING BEAN

SPICY BEAN BURGERS

These spicy bean burgers are naturally gluten-free and vegan.
They are really easy and speedy to whip up; great for a midweek dinner or a party!

120g mushrooms, chopped

120g carrots, sliced

10g flax

120g black-eyed beans

240g baked beans, mashed

120g kidney beans

40g tomato purée

20g BBQ sauce

1-2 tsp chilli powder

1 tsp salt

4 tsp paprika

16g gluten-free oats

2 tsp garlic powder

80g rice flour

19g fresh coriander, finely chopped

In a large bowl, combine the mushrooms, carrots and flax and then stir in the mashed baked beans. Wash the black-eyed beans and kidney beans then add these and all the remaining ingredients to the bowl. Mix everything until it binds together.

Divide the mixture into six and shape each piece into a burger patty. Place these on a baking tray lined with greaseproof paper and bake in the preheated oven for 45 to 50 minutes. Leave to cool, peel carefully away from the tray and then stack the burgers however you like!

Preparation time: 10 minutes | Cooking time: 45-50 minutes | Serves: 6

SHEFFIELD'S BEST-KEPT SECRET

Lembas is an independent workers' co-op that has been providing wholesale vegetarian and vegan foods to the north of England for over 35 years.

From its foundation in 1983 to its place in today's mainstream vegan market, Lembas has been committed to the principles of ethical trading, growing and recycling. The Sheffield-based co-op stands against the genetic manipulation of foodstuffs, and actively encourages the sale of organic goods by choosing suppliers who provide non-GMO products and supply a fully traceable certification. It also runs a food bank collection point for goods bought within or outside of Lembas, which enables deliveries to foodbanks in Sheffield.

Both trade and private customers come to Lembas for sustainable and ethical goods, which range from herbs and spices to sweets and chocolate. It stocks all kinds of beans, pulses, grains, cereals and sugars which are bagged into convenient sizes, as well as branded goods – including cupboard staples, exotic finds and plenty of vegan wines, spirits, beers and ciders – while household products and toiletries are also available. As a bulk supplier, the business uses considerably less packaging than you would generally find in retail, and ensures that what is used is either fully biodegradable or recyclable wherever possible.

Deliveries cover most of the north of England, and Lembas also has a thriving cash and carry service where anyone can shop and still benefit from wholesale prices. Wholefood shops, bakeries, caterers, schools, universities, hospitals, private individuals and buying groups or co-ops are amongst its diverse customer base. Supporting local ethical businesses is an important part of the ethos; most recently Lembas joined up with Sheffield Renewables – a social and community enterprise – to have solar panels fitted which now provide almost two thirds of a typical year's power, drastically reducing the business' impact on the environment.

As a workers' co-operative, decisions and skills are collective and shared, forming a close-knit team and a bustling, friendly atmosphere in the warehouse. Employee Russ says: "We all have a common goal: to continue and building on Lembas' success while running an environmentally conscious business, providing employment for us all and sticking to our shared ethical views of promoting a sustainable approach to food and life in general." From the business name – a Lord of the Rings reference – to advertising simply by word of mouth, Lembas has always done things its own way and customers who've stumbled on this Sheffield gem know that has always paid off!

LEMBAS
A FEW OF OUR PRODUCTS...

We stock many vegan and vegetarian products to feed your body and your lifestyle, and enjoy being able to showcase the best of the bunch from wonderful suppliers who share our commitment to ethical growing and sustainability.

Violife Cheeses

One of the major success stories in 2018, these 100% vegan cheeses are made from coconut oil and other ingredients to taste and act just like their dairy counterparts. Violife originated in Greece, and now offers a wide range of varieties; the mozzarella melts beautifully, the prosociano (a Parmesan-style block) flakes like the Italian original, and the flavours are perfect. Miracle workers! Violife has been named the top dairy-free cheese in The Grocer, is one of the top 20 best-selling cheese brands overall, and hit an 80% growth rate within a year. We can barely keep it on the shelves.

Faith in Nature

Faith in Nature has been making cosmetics since 1974. The business was founded in New York but then moved over to Scotland shortly after, and the products are now available all over the UK. Naturally-derived, cruelty-free, vegan ingredients are used to create luxuriant shampoos, conditioners and bubble bath, along with a great range of deodorants, soaps and skin care products such as the intensive moisturising cream and rejuvenating face wash.

Oat Milk

Another runaway success over 2018, oat milks are now probably our most popular non-dairy drink. The Swedish company Oatly do an organic one, a non-organic with added calcium, a chocolate and a rich creamy one, and now we can get Provamel's oat milk and barista oat milk. The new kid on the block is Minor Figures' barista-style offering, which is proving very popular with our café-owning customers. On top of all that we have soya milks, almond milks, rice milks, coconut milk drinks, hemp milk, tiger nut milk, and many more.

Beans, Pulses, Rice & Grains

Our absolute staples. Underpinning nearly every meal, we do a wide range of dry goods, several different lentil varieties, many kinds of rice, grains, and flakes or ready-made mueslis along with nuts, seeds and dried fruits to jazz them up a bit. 'Superfoods' have taken off too; we are based in what has become known as the 'quinoa quarter' of Sheffield! We also carry chia seeds, linseed, goji berries, aduki beans, acai berries and so on. All great products, and the basis of a well-stocked veggie or vegan cupboard.

TURNING OVER A
NEW LEAF

Coffee, kitchen, music: this tempting trio have transformed an historic public service building into Attercliffe's newest vegan-friendly hotspot.

The Library in Attercliffe, Sheffield was the brainchild of Justin Brooks – director, owner, chef, barman et cetera – who opened the venue in October 2018 to bring some glamour back to the city's overlooked 'East End'. The business is housed in a former library, hence the name, which was built in 1894 and still proudly displays many original features. As the first free library in Britain, its purpose was to serve the public and be a place for the local community. Justin has retained this as the driving ethos, bringing people together over fusion food and music for the soul.

The menu features tapas dishes inspired by cuisines from all over the world, all cooked fresh in the compact kitchen which used to be the librarian's office, yet can provide up to 160 guests with delicious locally sourced food and drink. A brand new selection of small plates, sandwiches and soups was unveiled in February 2019 with even more of a focus on vegan and gluten-free dining. For Justin, it's important to be open to change and embrace ways to cater for everybody. Ingredients or products supplied within the area, such as bread from Bakewell Bakery and cakes from the bakery next door, are hand-picked with a careful eye for top quality.

Drinks are no exception, with speciality gin and whisky behind the bar, fantastic cocktails on the menu and a partnership with Forge Coffee Roasters who freshly prepare the beans just across the road. The daytime café doubles up as a buzzing evening out on Tuesdays, Wednesdays and Thursdays when live music from local and global stars of the jazz, funk and soul world will perform. The venue is versatile thanks to its diverse past and has already hosted heritage events, book launches, private parties and other catered occasions with food especially made for vegans and gluten-free guests.

The future of Attercliffe's first free library has been secured by Justin's vision and passion for bringing exceptional food and drink, music and service together. He is keen to take the same model to other public spaces, creating community hubs and revitalising more forgotten areas for posterity.

CHICKPEA AND RED BEAN COCONUT CURRY

Having experienced more and more vegan customers coming to The Library, I realised that I needed to incorporate more vegan choices within my menu. This recipe, I developed with one of my regular vegan customers. It has the same great flavour as The Library's signature coconut chicken curry, with the substitution of chickpeas and red beans, and is becoming more and more popular with both our vegan and non-vegan customers.

3 tbsp coconut oil

2 white onions

3 cloves of fresh garlic

1 green capsicum pepper

1 yellow capsicum pepper

240g tin of chickpeas

240g tin of red kidney beans

½ tbsp paprika

1 tbsp ground cumin

1 tsp ground turmeric

2 tbsp mild madras-style curry powder (or hot, depending on your preference)

2 tins of coconut milk

Salt and pepper, to taste

Fresh coriander, to garnish

Place the coconut oil in a deep frying pan on a medium heat. While it warms up, peel and dice the onions and garlic, and deseed then chop up the peppers. Add the onion, garlic and peppers to the pan. Cook on a medium heat for 5 minutes.

Drain off the chickpeas and red beans, add them to the pan and cook for a further 5 minutes, tossing to ensure that the ingredients do not stick or burn. Add the paprika, cumin, turmeric, and curry powder and toss with the vegetables for 1 minute before adding both tins of coconut milk.

Simmer for 4 to 5 minutes, adding salt and pepper as required according to personal taste. While the curry cooks, wash the fresh coriander, removing the leaves from the stalks ready to garnish the dish.

Once the curry is cooked, leave to stand for 1 minute before garnishing with the fresh coriander and serving with your favourite side (rice, couscous or vegan flatbread all work well).

Preparation time: 15 minutes | Cooking time: 12-15 minutes | Serves: 4

WITH A LITTLE HELP FROM OUR FRIENDS

Little Vegan brings together plant-based and cruelty-free products, with plans for a café in the offing… Preston has been put on the vegan map by this food market with the health of people, animals and the planet at its heart.

Cooking was already a hobby for Little Vegan founder Carley, but having piqued fellow vegans' interest across social media with her food it soon became a small business. "I wanted to prove that vegan food wasn't boring," says Carley, "and had been experimenting with new flavours to create meals that were really just normal food 'veganised' for anyone to enjoy."

Little Vegan is now a thriving delivery-only takeaway and catering service in Preston. Customers place orders via social media or email for Carley's limited specials and weekly Wednesday breakfasts, which are all delivered directly to the customers. Additionally, Little Vegan attends the regular vegan markets with a street food style approach, and does outside catering for all events from corporate to weddings. As well as selling her own range of vegan meals, Carley sources great products – all organic and fresh where possible – from local independent producers, like Our Paula's and Vegannomnoms, and suppliers of vegan and cruelty-free products. They are referred to collectively by Little Vegan as 'our v friends' who together form a supportive network, aiming to help and promote the movement of plant-based eating.

Carley also makes her own mock meat to create burgers, steaks and VFC – that's vegan fried chicken, of course! – alongside her homely comforting dishes. Little Vegan supplies the on-site café at the University of Central Lancashire and has much bigger ambitions for the near future. With the Little Vegan flourishing, Carley is looking to crowdsource funds to open a café; people in Preston and the surrounding area are keen to enjoy the same food they can buy online as well as much more in what could be the town's first 100% vegan eatery.

Whatever direction her business moves in, the aim is to find ways of improving people's health, animal welfare and the state of the planet. "It's a win-win situation from my point of view," says Carley. "If you make the small change of switching your diet, you can create much bigger change."

VEGANNOMNOMS PRESTON

JALAPEÑO SCONES

Vegannomnoms was born out of Emma Robinson's love of cooking, and influenced by her volunteering at the local Buddhist centre. The small business began life in 2018 and is based at Emma's home in Preston, from which she bakes cakes and savouries like these spicy scones, creates vibrant salads and much more for event catering, she also hosts a monthly Secret Supper Club which features international cuisines. Vegannomnoms currently supplies a local pub and vegan supermarket, as well as taking cake orders for collection and catering for a wide variety of occasions with anything that's vegan and delicious!

375g flour
2 tbsp baking powder
2 tbsp brown sugar
1 tsp salt
¼ tsp black pepper
¼ tsp paprika
115g very cold vegan margarine
115g firm vegan cheese, grated
(I use the Violife Original Block)
250ml soya yoghurt
1 large jalapeño chilli, finely diced

Combine the flour, baking powder, sugar, salt, pepper and paprika in a large bowl and mix well. Cut in the margarine with a round-bladed knife until evenly distributed, then stir in the grated cheese. Cover the bowl and place in the freezer for 15 minutes.

Meanwhile, preheat the oven to 200°c and line a baking tray with greaseproof paper.

Once the mixture has chilled for 15 minutes, gently stir in the soya yoghurt and chilli. The dough will come together but will be sticky and shaggy-looking. Using a spoon in one hand, scoop out a portion of the dough, and using your spare hand shape it into a rough ball. Place the ball on the baking tray and press down lightly to make a scone shape. This will be messy so you may want to wear gloves! Repeat until you have 12 scones, all roughly the same size.

Bake the scones for 18 to 20 minutes on the middle shelf of the preheated oven until cooked all the way through. Serve at once! These are great with soup.

Preparation time: 10 minutes, plus 15 minutes chilling | Cooking time: 18-20 minutes | Makes: 12

OUR PAULA'S
FROM OUR KITCHEN TO YOURS...

We produce simply delicious veggie and vegan products for everyone to enjoy. Based in Chorley, Lancashire, we sell at markets and foody events as well as stocking awesome outlets dotted across the region. These include Leaf & Seed Wirral, The Bread Shop Bakery in Liverpool, Simply Vegetarian in Rawtenstall, The Glass Onion in Westhoughton, Barrons Farm Shop in Tarleton and Unicorn Grocery in Manchester. We can also post products to you via our Facebook page!

What's inside my little pots of loveliness (all good stuff!) ...

Our Paula's products are presented in glass pots to recycle or upcycle after use. They are all free from palm oil and contain no GMOs, just my secret blend of various ingredients such as certified coconut oil, soy lecithin, apple cider vinegar and turmeric, plus virgin olive oil, sea salt and more. They are all whizzed together with a giant spoonful of love, passion and dedication, creating so much more than just buttery spreads and pâté.

Garlic Butter

I have no favourites but this one was my first.... packed with fresh garlic and parsley, just taking the lid off will make your tastebuds do a happy dance! I use it in most of my cooking as it's so versatile. Spread on any bread then grill or oven-bake for amazing garlic bread, but garlic mushrooms are an absolute must, and it's fab with pasta or spuds too; the list is as long as your imagination!

Sea Salted Butter

My nemesis! After buying every vegan spread going, this took me forever to perfect, until I created a taste and texture that I enjoyed. Now it's my guilt-free pleasure on sourdough; simple bread and butter is pure comfort food but this is also heavenly on crumpets and scones.

Garlic & Chilli Butter

I don't do subtle so this one is hot with a lovely warm kick. Delicious with crackers and cheese, it also takes your mash to another level but only if it's not eaten straight from the pan! Chop and steam any leftover veg, add a dollop of this and wow: no more wasted veg.

Salted Caramel Butter

What can I say? I had to do something sweet, and love it or loathe it this flavour has to be in the line-up. Put this on crumpets, bagels, puddings, or just grab a spoon! The possibilities are endless; as my son says, drizzled over popcorn it's to die for!

Mushroom & Walnut Pâté

This is an amazing pot packed with mushrooms, walnuts, green lentils, lemon, beetroot, shallots and more. I take so much time and special care with every wonderful ingredient, roasting, sautéing, simmering and chopping before I send them to blender heaven. It's a long process but the end result completely justifies it; the flavour and texture means that one pot is never enough so my customers buy them in threes!

FOOD FOR
THOUGHT

An entirely vegan 'barcade' venue and a food menu designed to blow people's minds…what more could you want? There are plenty of hidden depths to Make No Bones at Church though, thanks to a unique and ever-evolving ethos that drives everything this innovative venture does.

Make No Bones at Church is a relatively recent addition to Sheffield's fun, inventive and diverse food scene. The shift from its previous incarnation as a small café to feeding up to 200 covers in a spacious bar and arcade has been a "massive learning curve" for Adam, Dave and Lauren who founded the business several years earlier. They were approached by Oli Sykes, a well known singer and entrepreneur, to work in collaboration with his new vegan venue, Church, which opened in July 2018 and is designed to support local businesses that work on the same ethos.

The Make No Bones kitchen serves up bar food from morning till late for hungry carnivores and committed vegans alike. Inclusivity is a founding principle of the business, meaning that while the edibles happen to be 100% vegan, that's not what people notice first about the burgers, loaded fries, salads, sandwiches, snacks and sweet treats proceeding from the hatch, ready to satisfy any craving without sacrificing things you love to eat. What they notice is the aroma, the flavour, the texture…in short, the food itself! "We're trying to pioneer plant-based food that people really want to eat," says Adam, "which means bringing quality back to the forefront and removing any stigma around veganism that can lead people to expect less of vegan food."

The trio spent six months developing the menu, testing it out on the lucky staff members at Drop Dead. Adam is a chef by trade but he, Dave and Lauren work in the kitchen collectively putting heart and soul into each dish. Some of the meat alternatives are made in-house to Make No Bones' own recipe, and it's always about striving for the best possible version of an ingredient or flavour combination.

For the team, it's not about what they do but why they do it. Clear vision and a journey-focused approach turns vegan food into a platform for limitless expansion, rather than the restrictive diet it can be perceived as. "We keep names like cheeseburger and pulled pork because it disarms any foregone conclusions and breaks down boundaries, "says Adam. "Food is the most commonly spoken language in the world – it might sound cheesy, but we believe it's absolutely true!"

AVOCADO WINGS WITH RANCH DIP

These wings are a signature dish down at MNB and have been featured on our menu from day one. The joy of this dish is that they actually turn out better with under-ripe avocados. So if you're stuck with a bunch of hard avos, this is a delicious and fast fail-safe way to make use of them. The ranch dip is one of my all-time favourite condiments and goes with so many other dishes, it's worth having a jar stored in the fridge at all times!

For the ranch dressing (makes 1 litre):
500ml high-quality soy milk
42g lemon juice
42g spirit vinegar
½ tbsp finely chopped fresh dill
½ tbsp sugar
½ tbsp garlic powder
½ tbsp onion powder
4 tbsp nutritional yeast
½ tsp salt
500ml sunflower oil

For the avo wings:
2 firm avocados, de-stoned and peeled
1 litre vegetable oil (for frying)

For the batter:
65g gram flour
35g soda water
½ tsp smoked paprika
⅓ tsp salt

To serve:
Sriracha sauce

For the ranch dressing
Combine all the ingredients (except the oil) in a deep container or large bowl. Using a stick blender, blitz everything together while gradually adding the oil. Make sure to incorporate the oil slowly to prevent splitting. If the dressing is too thin, continue to blend in more oil until the desired consistency is reached. You are looking for a smooth mayonnaise-like texture. Store in the fridge until required.

For the avo wings
Cut the peeled and de-stoned avocados into quarters. You should end up with 16 pieces. Pro tip: If you are not frying the wings straight away, dress the pieces of avocado with a little salt and lemon juice to prevent them from browning and store covered in the fridge.

For the batter
Combine all the ingredients and whisk thoroughly until smooth. Heat the oil to approximately 190°c.

To fry
Set up a tray lined with kitchen towel to drain off excess oil when the wings are removed from the fryer. Using tongs or a fork, gently drop the avocado pieces into the batter and ensure they are properly coated. It's usually best to do this in batches of four. Carefully lower the covered pieces into the oil one at a time. Fry for 5 minutes on either side, and remove when golden and crispy to the prepared tray so the oil can drain off. Repeat the above steps until all the wings are cooked.

To serve
Our favourite way of serving this dish is to stack up a heap of wings and drizzle them with the ranch dressing. For additional garnish, why not add Sriracha and chopped chives?

Preparation time: 10 minutes | Cooking time: 10 minutes | Serves: 4

THE
WHOLE WORLD IN
YOUR HANDS

Ethical and sustainable shopping is easy when somebody brings everything together in a vegan and vegetarian store right at the city's heart...

Out of this World can be nicely summed up by the double meaning in its name – something absolutely fantastic, and something to take us literally out of this world, towards positive change for the planet – but it is also much more than that. Established in Leeds city centre by owner Damian, the business was designed to be a one-stop shop for the whole spectrum of health foods. This holistic approach was paired with a convenient location to make Out of this World accessible to everyone: the opposite of niche hard-to-find places that rarely attract a diverse customer base.

People of all ages, backgrounds and interests – whether they are health food enthusiasts or casual shoppers passing by – can enjoy browsing Out of This World's well-stocked shelves and the special offers that make quality products affordable and good value. The size of the venue was important to Damian, as it meant being able to keep a large range always in stock so people know they can get everything in one place. The characterful building is in the oldest part of Leeds, just opposite the iconic Corn Exchange, and has provided the perfect spot since the shop's opening in 2003.

Damian started and continued Out of this World based on five core values that inform how and what the shop stocks. Organic, eco-friendly, Fairtrade, healthy and locally sourced: these are the cornerstones of the product range from the fruit and vegetables – which are all certified organic – to the cruelty-free bodycare. It also incorporates a vegan deli selling convenient but healthy takeaway food and wholesome options for lunch on the go, including sandwiches made daily on the premises using freshly baked bread from Otley favourite, Bondgate Bakery, and the Leeds Bread Co-Op.

All Out of this World's suppliers are based in Yorkshire, and in a time of so much innovation around vegan food and drink there's something new arriving on the shelves weekly. Specialist diet foods, milk alternatives, and the massive range of herbal teas always prove popular plus the options when it comes to organic, Fairtrade and vegan alcohol. "We're always looking to increase the amount of locally produced goods we can stock," says Damian, "because this is what sets us apart and why we're able, as a team, to have a genuine interest in everything we sell – we know where it came from and why it's great!"

OUT OF THIS WORLD
BANANA BLOSSOM FISH AND CHIPS

This exciting addition to the world of meat-free alternatives means you don't have to miss out on one of the nation's favourite dishes. Banana blossom has an amazing flavour which replicates the taste and texture of white fish, making it suitable for making your own homemade 'fish' and chips or 'fish' cakes!

For the 'fish':
2 tins (565g each) of banana blossom
500ml vegetable stock
2 tbsp lemon juice
2 tbsp seaweed flakes, plus extra for dusting
2 tsp salt
200ml white wine (optional)
Small bowl of plain flour

For the batter:
Vegetable oil, for deep frying
3 tsp baking powder
2 tsp salt
400g plain flour, chilled in the freezer for 15 minutes before use
550ml very cold vegan beer

'For the 'fish'

Drain and discard the liquid from the banana blossom and rinse gently but thoroughly. Take out the whole pieces of banana blossom and place them into a large bowl. Remove the smaller pieces (which have separated off) and set aside to use in another recipe such as a salad or stir fry.

Add the stock, lemon juice, seaweed flakes, salt and white wine if using to the bowl. Top up with hot water to make sure the banana blossom is just covered. Set aside for a minimum of 1 hour.

When thoroughly soaked, squeeze out the banana blossom pieces, being careful not to tear them. Dip them in the extra seaweed sprinkle and then in the plain flour.

For the batter

Half fill a large saucepan with vegetable oil and place on a medium heat until it reaches around 180°c. Just before frying, mix the baking powder and salt into the chilled flour, then whisk in the cold beer until you have a thick paste.

Completely cover each piece of banana blossom in the batter before lowering them into the hot oil. Don't overcrowd the pan. Cook for a few minutes or until golden brown and crispy. If the pieces stick to the bottom of the pan, make sure you detach them immediately or the batter will brown too quickly. Remove each piece with a slotted turner and place on kitchen roll to soak up the excess oil.

Serve with chips and peas!

Preparation time: 15 minutes, plus 1 hour soaking | Cooking time: 5-10 minutes | Serves: 4

G'DAY
SHEFFIELD!

Local produce, colourful food, a flair for décor and inventive dishes full of vegan and vegetarian goodness all come together at Pom Kitchen.

Pom Kitchen combines its owner's love for great food, beautifully designed interiors and eating out, in a fresh approach to breakfast, brunch and lunch. Zora grew up in Sheffield, but her partner spent most of his life in Sydney and so her first venture takes inspiration from Australia's burgeoning brunch scene and brings a vegan and vegetarian version of that lifestyle to the community of independents on Sharrow Vale Road.

Established in 2017 just a few doors down from her shop, Pom Kitchen is bright, colourful and buzzing seven days a week. Just as Zora envisaged from the beginning, its atmosphere is really relaxed, giving off a laid-back vibe that transports you to sunny beaches and cosmopolitan cities down under! Plenty of greenery trailing from wooden shelves overhead next to swirls of bright pink neon sets the look of the café apart. Zora's partner, a graphic designer, produces the artistic menu cards and Zora herself has paid attention to every aspect of Pom's interior from the energising colour scheme to — of course — the addition of a few pom-poms here and there.

It shouldn't come as a surprise that the most popular option from the food menu is a rainbow bowl full of colourful fresh ingredients. Fruit and vegetables are delivered every morning, forming the basis of the kitchen's creations for daily specials and regular favourites. Jaffles (an Australian toastie) always go down well too, which are made with Depot Bakery sourdough, and fresh eggs from Whirlow Hall Farm can be enjoyed knowing the hens' welfare is guaranteed. Local milk and butter — supplied by two more Sheffield producers, Our Cow Molly and Longley Farm — as well as cake and tea means there's something for everyone, any time of day.

Seasonal, health-conscious, mostly plant-based and full of flavour are the main criteria for Zora's food and drink. "If it hits all the spots and is super tasty, there's no need for a meat substitute, plus it has to be fun to eat and that's best for your body," she says. With Pom Kitchen full up most days — loved by both regulars and those new to meat-free dining — there are plans on the horizon to open a second venue in Sheffield city centre as part of a new food hall, open all day with the possibility of evening openings and a whole new dimension to explore in the neon-pink, Aussie-inspired, veggie and vegan world of better brunching.

SCRAMBLED TOFU ON TOAST

At Pom, scrambled tofu definitely isn't a substitute for egg. The texture is similar but this recipe is a deeply savoury, lightly spiced, totally moreish breakfast you'll want to make again and again!

Splash of oil

½ red pepper, diced

½ red onion, diced

Handful of cherry tomatoes, chopped

Handful of kale, shredded and stalks removed

Salt and pepper

1 fresh chilli or a pinch of chilli flakes

2 level tsp medium curry powder

100g firm tofu, crumbled (such as Tofoo)

50g smoked tofu, crumbled with your hands (we use Viana)

2 tbsp nutritional yeast

2 tbsp water

Heat the oil in a frying pan, then add the pepper, onion and tomatoes. Sauté together for 5 minutes on a medium heat. Add the shredded kale and season well. Continue cooking for a further 2 minutes so all the flavours can mingle.

Add the fresh or dried chilli, curry powder and both types of crumbled tofu to the pan. Stir everything together and turn the heat down slightly.

Stir through the nutritional yeast, followed by the water. Wait until the water has been soaked up and then pile the scrambled tofu onto freshly toasted sourdough drizzled with olive oil. Serve immediately. We love ours with sliced avocado!

Preparation time: 5 minutes | Cooking time: 10 minutes | Serves: 2

TRADITION
WITH A TWIST

On a foundation of family recipes from the Gujurati region of India, Prashad has built a reputation and inspired a widespread love of their unique take on tradition.

The Patel family have put all their passion and love of cooking and hospitality into Prashad since its first phase as a deli in Bradford. Kaushy and Mohan, parents of Bobby and Mayur, were looking for a change of lifestyle when the opportunity presented itself to take on a small local business. Thanks to some exceptional home cooking and big, warm, welcoming personalities the deli became very popular, acting as a stopgap for Gujurati Indians in the area who had struggled to find authentic produce, but soon embracing a much wider demographic as customers from all backgrounds realised how good this cuisine could be.

Prashad's team expanded when Bobby's wife joined the family; Minal was already a food lover and began by helping Kaushy in the kitchen, then eventually took on all the cooking. During this time, they were doing event catering alongside running the deli, but started to dip a toe into the restaurant industry as well, turning part of their deli venue into a small eatery. It was packed from the word go, gaining accolades and a strong following who loved what Prashad was doing with vegetarian food, most of which happened to be vegan, at a time when this was still unusual.

In 2010, Prashad was crowned runner-up in Gordon Ramsay's Best British Restaurant, and a couple of years later the restaurant's ever-increasing popularity enabled a move to new premises in Drighlington which have allowed the family to develop and expand Prashad exactly as they want. Today the restaurant is the only Bib Gourmand and two AA rosette establishment serving Indian food in Yorkshire, an achievement the family are very proud of. They love being recognised for the hard work each person puts in, from head chef Minal to operations manager (and full time dad) Bobby, whose brother Mayur co-owns Bundobust in Leeds and Manchester, drawing on his food heritage as Prashad does, spreading the love and good vibes instigated by their parents from the very beginning.

Quality food, integrity in their dishes, refinement, drawing on their culture and, most importantly, running the restaurant as a living, rather than simply by numbers, have been the keys to Prashad's success. The family doesn't take shortcuts and had big visions from the start, sharing their love of food, warmly welcoming customers, and enjoying the journey they're on!

RAMSAY'S BEST RESTAURANT

INDIAN

Prashad

Vegetable kofta,
jeera fried rice and baby bathura

Photograph: www.chapter81.co.uk

Prashad

PRASHAD

HARA BARA KEBABS

These patties are made with mashed peas and cauliflower along with spices and fresh aromatics, creating delicious bites of flavour that are great as a starter.

For the masala paste:

1-3 fresh green chillies (ideally Kenyan), trimmed but not de-seeded

1-2 cloves of garlic

2cm root ginger, peeled and roughly chopped

Pinch of salt

For the patties:

80g fresh or frozen peas

1 small red-skinned (or other waxy) potato

¼ head cauliflower, coarsely grated

¼ head cabbage, coarsely grated

½ medium-sized carrot, coarsely grated

1 handful of fresh coriander, rinsed and finely chopped

30g chapatti flour

30g rice flour

½ tsp garam masala

1 tsp salt

½ tsp black peppercorns, coarsely ground or crushed

1 tbsp lemon juice

Sunflower oil, for frying

Crush the chillies, garlic and ginger together with a pinch of salt using a pestle and mortar, or in a blender, to make a fine masala paste. Rinse the peas in warm water then chop with a sharp knife or in a blender until coarsely blended. Boil the potato in its skin, then peel and grate coarsely.

Put the masala paste, peas, grated potato and all the other ingredients except the sunflower oil in a large bowl. Mix thoroughly and combine to form a strong but workable dough-like paste. Lightly oil your hands and, taking three teaspoons of paste at a time, form the mixture into flattened round patties. Set aside on an oiled tray.

Heat about 15cm of sunflower oil in a large pan over a high heat (or in a deep fat fryer, if you have one) and when you think it is hot enough, test the temperature by dropping a little of the kebab mix in to the oil. When it is up to temperature, the mixture will quickly spring back up to float on the surface. Reduce the heat to medium at this point.

Gently lower four or five kebabs into the oil (or fewer, depending on the size of your pan). Use a heatproof spoon to move them around so that they cook evenly all over. Fry for 8 to 9 minutes or until dark brown with a crispy coating. Remove from the oil with a slotted spoon or strainer and leave to rest on absorbent kitchen towels while you fry the next batch. Repeat until all the kebabs have been fried.

If you are looking for a healthier alternative to deep-frying, you can oven-bake your hara bara kebabs, but note that they will have a rather more solid texture than the fried kebabs. Preheat the oven to 180°c and oil a baking tray. Place the uncooked kebabs on the tray, brush or spray with oil and cook for 1 hour, turning every 10 minutes to help them cook evenly.

Preparation time: 30 minutes | Cooking time: approx. 45 minutes | Serves: 4 (makes 12)

PRASHAD

BOMBAY BATAKA

This tamarind, tomato and potato curry uses a combination of sweet, sour and spicy ingredients to create layers of flavour. You can find tamarind in most Asian supermarkets, along with jaggery and asafoetida which is derived from the root of a herb in the same family as celery.

3 medium red-skinned (or other waxy) potatoes

25g dried tamarind (from a block)

600ml boiling water

3cm root ginger, peeled and roughly chopped

75ml sunflower oil

2-4 dried red chillies, snapped in half

1 tsp cumin seeds

1 tsp brown mustard seeds

¼ tsp asafoetida

400g tinned peeled plum tomatoes, finely chopped or blended

25g jaggery, cut into thin flakes (or soft brown sugar)

1 tsp medium red chilli powder

1 tbsp ground coriander

1½ tsp turmeric

1¼ tsp salt

2 handfuls of fresh coriander, rinsed and finely chopped

¾ tsp garam masala

Boil the potatoes in their skins for 40 minutes or so until a knife tip will slide in easily, then peel and cut into 2cm cubes. Meanwhile, soak the dried tamarind in 200ml of the boiling water for 10 minutes, then pulp with your fingers and sieve the tamarind water into a small bowl and set aside. Crush the ginger with a pestle and mortar, or in a blender, to make a fine pulp.

Heat the oil in a large pan for a minute over a medium heat before adding the dried red chillies, cumin and mustard seeds. When the mustard seeds start to pop, reduce the heat to low and stir in the asafoetida, blended tomatoes and jaggery. Stir over a low heat for a minute or so until the jaggery has dissolved.

Increase the heat to high and stir in the tamarind water, crushed ginger, chilli powder, ground coriander, turmeric, salt, half the fresh coriander and the remaining 400ml of boiling water. Cover and cook for 10 minutes to bring the spices together and intensify the flavours.

Add the garam masala and stir well; this is a strong flavour and needs to be thoroughly mixed in before you add the main ingredient. Stir in the potatoes gently to avoid breaking them up, then remove the pan from the heat, sprinkle with the remaining chopped coriander and leave to rest covered for at least 10 minutes to allow the flavours to infuse before serving.

MUNG DHAL KICHDI

*This soothing yellow lentil rice is a lovely accompaniment to many curries and other dishes,
especially our Bombay Bakata.*

175g mung dhal (yellow split mung
beans)
175g basmati rice
75ml sunflower oil
2-4 cloves of garlic, finely chopped
1 ¼ tsp salt
¼ tsp turmeric
900ml boiling water

Mix the dhal and rice together then rinse in warm water, running your fingers gently through to help clean them (and to check for small stones). Drain and repeat. Washing it twice removes enough starch to make the cooked rice fluffy and the grains separate.

Heat the oil in a large pan for 1 minute over a medium heat. Add the dhal and rice and fry together for 1 minute, gently stirring to coat them in oil. Stir in the garlic, salt and turmeric and fry for another minute, then pour in the boiling water. It is essential that the water is boiling as it helps the rice to cook quickly initially, which makes a big difference to the overall texture.

Bring to the boil, then simmer uncovered over a medium heat for 10 to 12 minutes until almost all the water has cooked off and it starts to look dry on top. Put a large square of aluminium foil on top of the rice and dhal, tucking it in to the edges of the pan to seal everything in and keep the rice moist and fluffy while it steams. Cover with the lid, reduce the heat to the lowest setting and leave to cook for 7 to 8 minutes. Remove from the heat and set aside to rest for at least 5 minutes.

When you remove the foil, everything should be perfectly cooked. Gently run a spoon through it to loosen, taking care not to break the rice grains, then serve straight away.

THE
SEED OF
AN IDEA

Shedding some light on health and happiness, alongside an inspiring menu of exciting food and drink, is the order of the day at a 100% plant-based café in Sheffield.

The evolution of Shed began with a passion for making health and wellbeing accessible through great food that's complex in design but simple by nature, literally! Entrepreneurs Gian and Joe co-founded the venture to offer everyone – whether they are vegan, vegetarian, flexitarian or the world's most committed carnivore – a step on the journey towards making better choices for themselves, starting with the concept that nourishment and deliciousness aren't mutually exclusive. The self-titled 'plant-pushers' are on a mission to inspire lifestyle changes that benefit mind and body without overwhelming or alienating anyone.

Creating a menu of food that excites and choices that inspire was a crucial stage of the process in developing the business. The team tested recipes and gathered feedback at events around Sheffield, and thanks to the talents of executive chef Carl and content creator Charlotte it all went down a treat. Having gauged demand (of which there was plenty) Shed then moved into a permanent home at Cutlery Works, the highly popular food hall, in November 2018. The café has a range of all-day dining options plus nibbles and guilt-free goodies all made entirely in-house, with drinks from cold-pressed juices to vegan wines sourced from suppliers as locally as possible.

"To say we do (amongst other things) salad bowls really doesn't do them justice!" says Gian. "Our whole ethos is based around demystifying plant-based nutrition and making it simple, accessible and enjoyable above all so that our customers experience something unique but not complicated. For us, however, there's so much thought and effort put into every component that you might be eating dozens of ingredients in one mouthful!" The upshot being, nothing is processed, there are no additives involved, refined sugars are nowhere to be seen and natural wholefoods reign supreme.

The everyday approach to nutrition and all-round wellness extends beyond the café for Shed, whether that means hosting wellness weekends, providing free recipes, doing talks in workplaces or collaborating with local fitness and lifestyle companies. The team's ambition and vision is continually expanding, connecting what they do now to what can be done in future, funnelling information to people and championing healthier choices, with a passion for plant-based goodness at heart.

COCO LOCO DESSERT POT

Whipping up a plant-based dessert with added 'wow' factor takes no time. This has proven to be a real favourite with Shed customers and now you can make it at home! Combining organic soya milk and rich cacao chocolate with a few other healthy ingredients, this treat is truly guilt-free.

350ml organic soya milk
250g sweet potato purée
70g dates, pitted
50ml water
¼ tsp pink salt
130g 100% cacao chocolate
Coconut and banana chips

Blend it up
Put the organic soya milk, sweet potato purée, pitted dates, water, and pink salt into a blender. Blend it all up until you have a smooth consistency.

Get melting
Melt the 100% cacao chocolate. Add it to the blender and blend the mixture once again.

Cool it down
Divide the mixture into pots and put them in the fridge to set for around three hours or overnight.

Get serving
To serve, remove the pots from the fridge and add the coconut and banana chips to the top of the dessert.

Preparation time: 20 minutes | Chilling time: 3 hours | Serves: 5-6

A
STEP AHEAD

Relaxed, friendly, honest and locally inspired: these are the words that sum up Shoe Tree Café,
whose unusual name nods to an unusual spectacle in their local park…you guessed it, a tree
adorned with shoes!

Joe Carr-Hollands and Nina Wesolowski were teachers before starting their own venture, but having had an eclectic range of jobs already – including youth work, establishing a community garden, bar work and pot washing following creative degrees in fine art and film – the couple did not bat an eyelid when the opportunity arose to take over a café at the end of their street. They quit their jobs, bought the business, got pregnant, and all of a sudden Shoe Tree Café and their first baby were born within months of each other.

The aim was always to provide reasonably priced, tasty, homemade vegan and veggie food, as well as creating a space for cosy and interesting events such as life drawing, local music nights, pop up evening meals, knitting groups, art exhibitions, performance art and more! The space was transformed by their own hands with help from friends and family; tables and countertops were fashioned from locally sourced beech and ash trees, and they also built a mini kitchen for little ones to play in.

From the grown-ups' kitchen, Big Vegan Breakfast is the firm favourite. The vegan cakes are also big winners; the spiced vanilla chai always goes in a day! Menu inspiration comes from travelling around the UK, Europe and North America. For example, the 'Hail Seitan Sandwich' was inspired by Montreal smoked meat sandwiches, and the 'TLT' pays homage to Joe and Nina's favourite sandwich from Stereo in Glasgow.

"I think we left a piece of our hearts in Glasgow when we moved back to Tyneside," says Nina, "so we use a Glasgow-based ethical cooperative wholesaler and tea shop, but our coffee is roasted in Tynemouth, our bread is baked in Byker, the sweet treats are made by our neighbour and most other things are made in-house. We are always working towards an ethical low-impact menu."

Alongside a very close-knit team, Joe and Nina have had a whirlwind so far with Shoe Tree Café. "It's the sum total of lots of love, hard graft, good people and loyalty", they explain. "It's an extension of us, our values and I guess a bit like an extension of our living room (baby included), so as we grow, as will the café…"

BREAKFAST BEANS

These beans are regularly commented on by our customers as being one of the highlights of our breakfast menu. They find a lovely balance between being sweet, smoky and salty and are enjoyed by both adults and bairns alike. They're super easy to whip up and freeze really well.

1 tbsp oil

1 medium-sized white onion, finely chopped

3 cloves of garlic, crushed

500g passata

1½ tbsp tomato purée

1½ tbsp soy sauce

500g (about 2 tins, drained) pinto or borlotti beans

1 tsp smoked paprika

1 tsp dried thyme

1½ tbsp brown sugar

1 tsp black pepper

½ tsp salt

Heat the oil in a pan over a medium heat and add the onion. Cook for around 8 minutes until the onion is soft and translucent. Add the garlic and cook for a further 2 minutes.

Once the onions and garlic are cooked, turn the heat down to low. Add the passata, purée and soy sauce and mix well. Add the rest of the ingredients and stir. Continue stirring until the mixture begins to bubble.

Serve on a couple of slices of sourdough toast or as an accompaniment to your vegan full English breakfast.

Preparation time: 10 minutes | Cooking time: 15 minutes | Serves: 6 (generous portions)

SOUTH STREET SUNSHINE

Park Hill is Sheffield's most iconic estate, a monument of concrete and glass overlooking the hills of the city. Now there's even more reason to visit, thanks to the vibrant Middle Eastern flavours and bright, welcoming spaces of South Street Kitchen.

Creating a laid-back and sustainable café for the local community and beyond is both a motivation and a firm commitment for the co-owners of South Street Kitchen. Rachel and Tim fell in love with the venue during a visit to an art exhibition next door, in the old pub The Scottish Queen. Surrounded by greenery, filled with light through expansive windows, away from the traffic and noise of the city below; this idyllic setting, only a few minutes' walk from Sheffield's train station, forms a lovely contrast to the famous Brutalist architecture of Park Hill.

Such unusual qualities are what attracted former lawyer Rachel to the building, and she took the opportunity to create a space for the community, events, visitors and meetings…in short, a place that welcomed everybody. The menu reflects that approach, with an understanding of and flexible options for allergies, including gluten intolerance, and freshly prepared food by chefs Nicky and Michael, which covers an amazing variety of textures and flavours. Rachel's travels in Palestine informed her love of numerous Middle Eastern cuisines, which inspire the vegetarian and vegan dishes from soups and salads to tagines and falafel.

Breakfast and lunch are served Monday to Saturday, and Friday evenings are always buzzing with themed food and cocktails, wines, or northern craft beers. Any day of the week is a day for coffee, though, thanks to Yorkshire-based speciality roaster and barista training school Dark Woods, from whom South Street Kitchen sources and serves the perfect brew. Buying ethically and working sustainably – while keeping the café accessible and affordable to all – is really important to the team. This means supporting other local independent businesses and using suppliers who share their ethos to buying organic produce wherever possible. On the retail side, South Street Kitchen is plastic-free, and also avoids chemical-based cleaning as a general rule to further protect the environment.

Rachel and Tim aim to create a relaxed and beautifully designed environment for the community and others to enjoy. Without using any obvious labels which might be exclusive, they want the venture to be inclusive in all respects, welcoming everyone with freshly cooked produce.

SOUTH STREET KITCHEN

MAQLUBA

This dish is our interpretation of a Middle Eastern family favourite which makes an ideal centrepiece at any occasion. Magluba means upside down as the dish is turned between wooden boards at the table. This dish is very flexible and can include any of your favourite seasonal vegetables.

2 large aubergines
Rapeseed oil
Salt and pepper

For the rice:
1½ tsp cumin
1 white onion, diced
2 cloves of garlic, crushed
2½ cm piece of ginger, peeled and grated
150g basmati rice
3 strands of saffron, soaked in 15ml warm water

For the sauce:
2 tsp cumin, toasted until fragrant
1 tsp ground coriander
1 tsp ground cinnamon
½ tsp ground turmeric
1½ tsp sea salt
3 cloves of garlic, crushed
2 red onions, diced
1 red pepper, diced
½ red chilli, deseeded and finely chopped
400g plum tomatoes, crushed
400g tinned chickpeas, drained

To assemble:
3 sprigs of thyme
3 vine tomatoes, sliced
½ head of cauliflower, florets sliced
Toasted almonds

Preheat the oven to 200°c while you dice the aubergines into 2½ cm cubes. Spread them out on a baking tray, drizzle lightly with rapeseed oil, sprinkle with salt and pepper, then bake for 15 to 20 minutes until golden.

For the rice

Meanwhile, fry the cumin in a tablespoon of rapeseed oil until fragrant before adding the onion, garlic and ginger. Cook over a medium heat with a lid on until translucent but not coloured. Add the rice and cook for approximately 1 minute, until the grains have absorbed the spiced oil. Add 150ml of water and the soaked saffron. Bring to the boil, cover with a lid, remove from the heat and allow to steam with the lid on for 10 minutes.

For the sauce

Fry the spices in two tablespoons of rapeseed oil until fragrant before adding the salt, garlic and red onions. Cook over a medium heat until the red onions are lightly caramelised, then add the red pepper and chilli. Continue to cook for a few more minutes until the pepper has softened. Add the plum tomatoes (removing any remaining skin) and the drained chickpeas; simmer for 5 minutes until thickened.

To assemble

Lightly oil a casserole dish and scatter the thyme sprigs across the bottom (this will be the top of the magluba when you serve it). Make a layer of the sliced tomatoes, surround them with the raw cauliflower, cover with half of the tomato and aubergine sauce followed by the saffron rice before finally adding the remaining tomato sauce.

Press down lightly, cover and bake at 180°c for 30 minutes until firm. Allow to rest for a few minutes at room temperature before turning over between two wooden serving boards.

To serve, top the magluba with toasted almonds and accompany with fresh salads, lemon wedges, olives and your choice of plant-based yoghurt.

Preparation time: 30 minutes |Cooking time: 30 minutes |Serves: 6-8

SIMPLY
DELI-ICIOUS!

Inspired menus and creativity in the world of plant-based food are what Sunshine Deli do best, catering for events and serving up street food across Sheffield.

Sunshine Deli has been providing Sheffield with totally plant-based goodness in the form of healthy, traditional and comfort food since March 2018. Founded by Sarah Short, the venture has expanded into catering, deliveries and events alongside the deli itself on Penistone Road.

As the name promises, working with Sunshine Deli is always a positive experience whether you and your dog are popping in for coffee and cake, or you have a team of boxers to feed. "When it comes to food I'm very influenced by my Nan," says Sarah. "I've always been a feeder – I love to make good food for people – and we have a great environment here in the deli. A lot of customers say it's like sitting in someone's kitchen! So it's homely and comforting, which is also how we like our food."

The options vary from 'Full Monty' breakfasts to Yorkshire pudding wraps and pizzas, all vegan and all made with quality produce that Sarah and her partner (both in life and business, who is also named Sarah) like to source locally, where possible, in order to support other small independents. As much of the products as possible are homemade at the deli, including a range

of mayonnaise featuring mustard, chilli, mint, and garlic varieties. They also supply their food to other venues, such as their delicious 'Southern Fried Zinger Chicken' to The Incredible Nutshell.

Sticking to their motto of 'real food made by real people' means the two Sarahs and their team only create what they are passionate about. "The menu is quite fluid," says Sarah, who is still the head cook as well as general manager and multi-tasker, "and it changes seasonally though the specials are weekly so we can mix it up more often."

Sunshine Deli is already a familiar face at events and venues across the city such as Sheffield O2 Academy, Little Wolf Events, Vegan Food Festivals. Yellow Arch Studios, the University of Sheffield, Abbeydale Brewery and Tramlines, as well as local markets where freshly made street food is the main attraction. The catering side of the venture is varied and always expanding; Sarah will soon be working with a nutritionist to create meals for professional boxers and is in the process of creating CFC – cruelty-free chicken – for the deli. Watch this space!

HOISIN MOCK DUCK SPRING ROLLS WITH EGGY TOFU FRIED RICE

I love to make this dish at the deli, and it's often on our menu as a special. What's mock duck, I hear you ask? Well, it's made of wheat gluten, oil, sugar, soy sauce and salt, and is a cruelty-free way to enjoy a traditional Chinese favourite.

1 pack of spring roll pastry
1 banana, peeled
Vegetable oil

For the filling:
300g mock duck
½ tsp salt
1 leaf of Chinese leaf lettuce, finely sliced
½ onion, finely sliced
A handful of coriander, finely sliced
2 spring onions, finely sliced
1 red pepper, finely diced
1 tbsp hoisin sauce

For the marinade:
½ tbsp light soy sauce
1 tbsp sweet chilli sauce
1 tbsp sesame oil
1 tbsp hoisin sauce
½ tsp dark soy sauce

For the 'eggy' fried rice:
300g cooked white rice
150g garden peas
150g sweetcorn
2 tsp soy sauce
1 tbsp sweet and sour sauce
100g tofu
2 tsp turmeric
½ tsp black salt
2 tbsp nutritional yeast

Start by preparing to make the spring rolls. Carefully separate each of the spring roll pastry sheets and stack them before covering with cling film.

For the filling

Place a frying pan onto a medium-high heat and cook the mock duck with a dash of oil for around 6 minutes. Set the mock duck aside to cool, then finely chop and mix with all the remaining filling ingredients. Combine all the ingredients for the marinade, then stir the filling in to completely coat everything.

To wrap the spring rolls, take the first sheet from the stack prepared earlier and use the banana to create a line of 'glue' along the edge. Turn the sheet so one of the corners is facing you, place a spoonful of filling onto the sheet and start to roll it away from you, starting from the nearest corner. When you have rolled half way into the middle, fold the two sides into the centre and then run the banana around the remaining edges. Roll away again to create the classic spring roll shape, sticking the edges down with banana.

To cook the spring roll, half fill a wok with vegetable oil and heat to 170°c or until you have done the chopstick test. The chopstick test determines if the oil is hot enough, indicated by a hissing sound when you dip a wooden chopstick into the oil for 2 to 3 seconds. When the oil is hot enough, carefully add the spring rolls to the wok, no more than 10 at a time, and deep fry until they have turned crispy and golden. Use a slotted spoon to remove them then leave to drain on kitchen paper.

For the 'eggy' fried rice

Mix the cooked rice with the peas, sweetcorn, soy sauce and sweet and sour sauce. For the 'eggy' part of the rice, squeeze the tofu between your fingers so it looks like scrambled egg. Fry the tofu and stir in the turmeric, black salt and nutritional yeast. Add the cooked rice mixture to the tofu in the pan and fry on a high heat with a little oil.

To serve

Plate up the spring rolls on a bed of 'eggy' fried rice then drizzle hoisin sauce over the top. Enjoy!

Preparation time: 1 hour | Cooking time: 15 minutes | Makes 8-10

LIFE IS
WHAT YOU
BAKE IT

With compassion and kindness at its core, The Tasty Vegan Food Company
offers just what its name suggests, from an ethical and spiritual foundation.

Tripatpal Kaur completely changed career in 2016 when she decided to expand her love of baking into a small catering business. Compassion for her fellow creatures has always been an important part of her Sikh faith, so vegan was an obvious lifestyle choice. Her niece's wedding, with a couple of hundred guests to feed, was the company's first big event. Its first stockist was a café in Sunderland that had to double check Pal's creations were completely plant-based, as the owner couldn't taste the difference!

The company's reputation for tasty vegan foods built very quickly. Pal now supplies many cafés and private customers with cakes and savoury products, including authentic Indian foods. Pal reveals that the secret behind her tasty food is the positive energy that goes into it, as much as the ethical ingredients. She is a great believer in the old saying that cooking with love provides food for the soul.

As a young girl, Pal was taught how to cook by an amazing lady who had a massive influence on her life. At a time when it was not so easy for women, Bibi Balwant Kaur ji MBE was a loving soul who used to collect and take aid to disaster zones around the world, personally comforting and helping thousands of people. She was like a second mother to Pal, and alongside traditional cooking skills, taught her that the vibes that surround food also go into that food. So Pal has always made sure that she cooks in a joyful environment, where there are only positive vibes. For her, baking has become almost like a form of meditation.

For Pal, veganism means taking a loving approach to life in all its forms, including kindness and compassion towards other humans as well as animals. She does not believe in judging others on their progress towards a sustainable lifestyle for the planet, as everyone is at a different stage in this journey. Running a business from home means that Pal has worked hard to find balance between her four children and all the elements of her company, with support from her husband.

So, when you buy The Tasty Vegan Food Company's sweet or savoury treats in a café, or use their catering service, you're getting more thoughtful food – and perhaps food for thought – than you might think!

PREET'S MANGO STRAWBERRY TART

My daughter Preet is a lover of all things mango and strawberry! She would spend our supermarket trips eyeing up the strawberry tarts in the fridge section, with all the patisserie. I wanted her to know that just because she had decided to become a vegan didn't mean she had to give up treats that she loved and enjoyed so much. She was my inspiration for this recipe.

For the pastry:
250g plain flour
Pinch of salt
75g hard block vegan margarine
75g vegetable shortening
10ml really cold water

For the mango custard:
70g sugar
50g custard powder
1 tsp Vege-Gel
200ml soya milk
500ml canned mango pulp
330ml single soya cream

For the topping:
1 large ripe mango or canned sliced mango
8-10 fresh strawberries
1 twin pack Green's Red Quick Jel
½ tsp strawberry flavouring or extract
400ml water
50g sugar

For the pastry

Combine the flour and salt, then rub the margarine and shortening into the flour until it resembles breadcrumbs. Bring the mixture together with cold water and wrap the pastry in cling film. Rest in the fridge for 30 minutes. Roll out to cover a 25cm flan or pie dish, then bake for 25 to 30 minutes at 200 to 220°c.

For the mango custard

Mix the sugar, custard powder and Vege-Gel into the soya milk in a small jug. In a saucepan, heat up the mango pulp and soya cream. While stirring, add the sugar mixture to the heated mango pulp and cream. Bring to the boil and simmer while stirring for 1 minute. Pour into the baked tart crust and place in the fridge for 30 minutes.

For the topping

Slice the fresh mango and strawberries and arrange on top of the set custard. In a saucepan, combine the Quick Jel, strawberry flavouring or extract, water and sugar. Bring to the boil and simmer for 1 minute. Cool while stirring for 3 to 4 minutes and then pour onto the fresh fruit. Place in the fridge to set for a further 30 minutes.

Serve the tart with whipped dairy-free cream if you like.

Preparation time: approx. 2 hours 30 minutes | Cooking time: 45 minutes | Serves: 8-10

SAY
CHEASE!

*The cheeseboard of the future is now a reality thanks to the invention
of one cheese-loving vegan family…*

Tyne Chease is a small family-run business producing a unique range of plant-based raw vegan cheese that's good for you and your taste buds! The artisan products are made with a few simple ingredients then cultured and matured in just the same way as traditional cheeses. The result is a perfect wheel of firm chease or pot of creamed chease, ideal for 'the cheaseboard of the future' or simply indulging, whether you're lactose intolerant, vegan, or want to cut down on cholesterol.

Cashew or macadamia nuts are the key ingredient for the cheases, simply combined with water, salt and vegan probiotics. They are flavoured with an eclectic selection of exotic spices such as za'atar and Ethiopian spice which Ami was inspired to use by living abroad before settling in Tyneside. The mini wheels of firm chease are boxed and there's also a variety of flavoured creamed chease packaged in little glass jars. The product that still sets them apart, though, is the Tyne Chease selection box which includes 10 tiny tasters for those who can't decide which one is their favourite, or anyone dipping their toe into the world of vegan cheese.

Ami and James Deane are the couple behind the venture, which has scooped several awards nominations since it began, and won the Vegan Festival award for Best Vegan Cheese in 2016. Having started to experiment with non-dairy cheeses as a teenager, wanting to create something for her cheese-loving vegan mum, Ami started trading in June 2015. She became a familiar face at nearly all vegan food festivals across the North and it was clear people loved the new concept, so Tyne Chease developed an online presence to broaden its reach and was contacted by health food shops wanting to stock the range.

Today, more than 90 wholesalers in the UK, France and Belgium stock a variety of firm and soft chease made by Ami and James. "The business was absolutely driven by demand," explains the entrepreneurial pair, "and has grown as organically as possible, which is great because we know people really love what we do." Three full time staff and a baby boy have since joined the team of two, who are hoping to acquire new premises in 2019 and continue expanding with new flavours, more vegan festivals, online sales and their ever-increasing stockist list!

Food Allergy Notice

Please be advised
that these products
contain **Nuts** and

Food Allergy Notice

Please be advised
that these products
contain **Nuts** and

Artisanal
Cheese Wheel
£7.9F

TYNE CHEASE
ARTISANAL CULTURED & AGED CASHEW NUT PRODUCT
100% PLANT BASED · RAW · APPROX. 150g
PINK PEPPERCORN
HAND MADE IN THE NORTH EAST OF ENGLAND

TYNE CHEASE LTD
ARTISANAL CULTURED & AGED CASHEW NUT PRODUCT
VEGAN · RAW · 150g
CRANBERRY
HAND MADE IN THE NORTH EAST OF ENGLAND

TYNE CHEASE LTD
ARTISANAL CULTURED & AGED CASHEW NUT PRODUCT
VEGAN · RAW · 150g
ZA'ATAR SPICE
HAND MADE IN THE NORTH EAST OF ENGLAND

TYNE CHEASE LTD
ARTISANAL CULTURED & AGED CASHEW NUT PRODUCT
VEGAN · RAW · 150g
CHIVES
HAND MADE IN THE NORTH EAST OF ENGLAND

TYNE CHEASE LTD
ARTISANAL CULTURED & AGED CASHEW NUT PRODUCT
VEGAN · RAW · 150g
SMOKED
HAND MADE IN THE NORTH EAST OF ENGLAND

TYNE CHEASE
ARTISANAL CULTURED NUT PRODUCT
100% PLANT BASED · RAW · APPROX 150g
MACADAMIA TRUFFLE
HAND MADE IN THE NORTH EAST OF ENGLAND

TYNE CHEASE LTD
ARTISANAL CULTURED & AGED CASHEW NUT PRODUCT
VEGAN · RAW · 150g
ORIGINAL
HAND MADE IN THE NORTH EAST OF ENGLAND

TYNE CHEASE LTD
ARTISANAL CULTURED & AGED CASHEW NUT PRODUCT
VEGAN · RAW · 150g
TRUFFLE
HAND MADE IN THE NORTH EAST OF ENGLAND

TYNE CHEASE
ARTISANAL CULTURED & AGED CASHEW NUT PRODUCT
100% PLANT BASED · RAW · APPROX 150g
GARLIC

TYNE CHEASE LTD
VEGAN · 150g
ORIGINAL
HAND MADE IN THE NORTH EAST OF ENGLAND

TRUFFLE

TYNE CHEASE
FONDUE

Vegan fondue is not only possible, it's pretty darn easy and incredibly delicious to boot! Smooth, creamy, and so luxurious…you'll want to dip everything in this stuff. Don't limit yourself to only using our Original Creamed Chease; why not get adventurous and try our other flavours, such as Smoked, Garlic or Chive.

215g jar of Tyne Chease Original Creamed Chease
250ml vegan white wine
250ml vegetable stock
1 clove of garlic, minced
1 tsp wholegrain or Dijon mustard
1 tsp white miso paste
A pinch of nutmeg
A pinch of black pepper

For dipping:
Crusty sourdough bread
Lightly steamed vegetables
Apple or pear slices

If you are using an electric fondue pot, turn it up to a medium heat. Otherwise place a saucepan over a medium heat.

Place the white wine, 200ml of the stock, the garlic, mustard and miso in the pot or pan and whisk to combine everything thoroughly. Once the mixture is warm, put the Original Creamed Chease in a bowl and gradually add 50ml of the heated liquid to the chease until it feels thinner. Now add the creamed chease mixture to the pan of liquid ingredients and whisk until smooth and bubbly. You can add the remaining stock to thin out the mixture as required.

Season with the nutmeg and black pepper, and then enjoy with bread and vegetables of your choice! This vegan chease fondue is a great and fun way to gather friends and family together, perfect for a summer barbecue or a cosy night in by the fire.

GOOD
FOOD
FOR ALL

Unicorn Grocery is a worker-owned business, inspired by co-operative principles and full of produce from organic, ethical and environmentally-friendly sources.

Over the last 23 years a pioneering and passionate worker's co-operative has grown in the South Manchester community of Chorlton. Unicorn is driven by the values of it's Principles of Purpose and members work collectively to trade in a better way while keeping produce affordable for customers. The shelves speak for themselves, they are stocked with the grocer's entirely plant-based range: fresh fruit and vegetables, store cupboard essentials, household and body care products, beer and wine, chilled and frozen items, pre-prepared foods and deli counter delights made in the purpose-built kitchen above the shop floor.

Since its small beginnings, Unicorn Grocery has focused on affordable quality ingredients to provide customers with the foundations for healthy, tasty and seasonal eating. The shop can now compete with big-name supermarkets in size and range; its values have enabled growth from a membership of 4 to over 70, created opportunities for the purchase of and renovations to the building, and earned the venture its second title of Best Food Retailer at the 2017 BBC Food and Farming Awards.

The staff are motivated by their collective mission: to solve a problem in the food industry by providing a thriving example of alternative business model and decent livelihoods, encouraging sustainable farming, enabling good health through good food and creating community wealth. They are proud to be part of a tradition of co-operatives which began with the Rochdale Pioneers in the 1800s and continues through Unicorn's Grow a Grocery scheme, helping others to create alternatives to supermarkets across the UK.

Project work offering financial support to communities in the UK and farther afield is a key part of Unicorn's Principles of Purpose, as is a more sustainable kind of trade. To this end Unicorn cultivates stronger links with suppliers and growers, such as Glebelands City Growers, Unicorn's most local supplier. This nearby market garden provides salad leaves, herbs, winter veg, and plants to take home which are all sold in the grocery. Unicorn's members like to work with innovators like Glebelands; as well as cutting food miles they use organic methods to reduce environmental impact.

This long-term commitment to wholesome food and a holistic approach to people and produce has made Unicorn a hub in the community, somewhere that customers feel proud of and stay loyal to for years as part of a bigger and friendlier solution to eating and living well.

SPLIT PEA TARKA DHAL WITH CRISPY ONIONS

Dhal is a lovely, comforting dish that can be eaten year-round. It is super easy, nutritious and cheap and can be made with any pulses you have in your cupboard! We use UK-grown yellow split peas from the lovely Hodmedods, or red lentils which cook in about half the time. Experiment with different spices, add greens towards the end of cooking, throw in a tin of coconut milk, or add a lump of creamed coconut: you really can't go wrong here!

400g yellow split peas

2 tsp ground turmeric (or a thumb-size piece of fresh turmeric, finely grated)

1 tsp asafoetida (optional)

Handful of cherry tomatoes, halved

For the crispy onions:

300ml rapeseed or sunflower oil

2 large onions, peeled and sliced

For the tarka:

2 medium onions

2 tbsp oil from the crispy onions

4 cloves of garlic

A thumb-size piece of ginger

2 tsp cumin seeds

1 tsp black mustard seeds

1 tsp chilli flakes

To finish:

Small bunch of fresh coriander

1 tsp salt (or to taste)

Soak the split peas for 2 hours (or overnight) then rinse thoroughly in cold water. Soaking the split peas reduces the cooking time, but it's not essential, so give dry split peas an additional 20 to 30 minutes of cooking time to make sure they're really soft.

Put the split peas in a large pan with 1 ½ litres of cold water. Place on a high heat until boiling and skim off any scum that floats to the surface. Add the turmeric, asafoetida and tomatoes to the pan. Turn down to a simmer and cook with a lid just resting on the pan (so the steam can escape) for 50 minutes to 1 hour, stirring occasionally. The split peas should then be completely soft.

For the crispy onions

Prepare these while the dhal is cooking. Heat the oil in large frying pan. When hot add half the onions and cook, stirring occasionally, until dark golden in colour. Remove with a slotted spoon and drain on kitchen paper or a wire rack. Repeat with the other half. It is necessary to use a lot of oil to make the onions crisp up. Reuse some of this for the tarka (no need to wash the pan) and save the rest for the next time you fry onions.

For the tarka

Halve the onions and slice them finely. Heat the oil in a frying pan and cook on a medium heat for 15 minutes, stirring occasionally, until soft and golden. Finely chop the garlic and ginger, or blend in a little oil. Add them to the onions along with the cumin and mustard seeds and the chilli flakes. Fry for a couple more minutes until the seeds start to pop, then stir the tarka through the dhal.

Stir the dhal really well so that the peas break down and it gets nice and creamy. If it is too thick, add water, if too thin cook uncovered for a while longer.

To finish

Add salt to taste. Chop the coriander, including the stalks unless they are woody, keep a small amount back for garnish and stir the rest through the dhal. Serve with coriander and crispy onions piled on top of each bowl.

Preparation time: 15 minutes, plus 2 hours soaking | Cooking time: approx. 1 hour | Serves 4

COURGETTE SALAD WITH LEMON AND ALMONDS

This is a lovely zingy salad. Perfect for a hot day and a great way of using up the endless supply of courgettes that the summer brings! Ours come from Glebelands City Growers just down the road in Sale and we have this dish on our deli counter most days through peak courgette season. It's still lovely without the preserved lemon, and if you don't have coriander you can substitute it with basil or just use mint; feel free to play around with combinations and enjoy being creative.

50g flaked almonds
Handful of fresh mint
Small bunch of fresh coriander
1 lemon
1 fresh chilli or a pinch of chilli flakes
4 smallish courgettes
60ml (4 tbsp) extra-virgin olive oil
1 preserved lemon (optional)
Sprinkle of sumac (optional)

Heat a frying pan and toast the almonds for a couple of minutes, stirring often. Keep a close eye on them as they burn easily. When they are starting to colour and smell delicious tip onto a plate and leave to cool. Pick through the herbs and remove any woody stems. Set aside some for garnish. Grate the zest of the lemon and set aside, then squeeze the juice out. With a stick blender, combine the herbs, oil and lemon juice. If you don't have a blender just chop everything up finely and mix it with a fork. Slice the chilli finely and add this or the flakes to the dressing. Chop the preserved lemon into small pieces, not forgetting to remove any pips. Slice the courgettes finely using a food processor if you have one, or a spiralizer. You could use a peeler to slice ribbons lengthways, or just slice with a sharp knife, as thinly as possible.

To assemble the salad, mix the dressing and preserved lemon through the courgettes, divide onto plates and scatter the toasted almonds over the top. Sprinkle with sumac and garnish with fresh herbs. If you are not using preserved lemon you may want to add a small pinch of salt.

EAT PLANTS,
HAIL SEITAN

If you've ever been served a Portobello mushroom in a bun and been assured that it is, in fact, what passes for a vegan burger then V Rev is here to challenge that notion.

Dom opened V Rev (then V Revolution) back in 2011 as a punk and hardcore record store that sold a few bits of vegan food, backed by a belief that this way of eating shouldn't be dull or inaccessible. The business built up a following one menu item at a time, gaining popularity with people still craving a cheeseburger without wanting to sacrifice their ethics. The offering soon expanded to include diner-style food from hotdogs to milkshakes.

Fast forward to now and the venture serves up award-winning, hand-crafted vegan food seven days a week. It's also a licensed venue, with vegan beers, wines and classic cocktails on the menu. V Rev's popularity enabled the move to larger premises in 2016, where the décor is bright and colourful, art by friends and local talents adorns the walls, and a laid-back, welcoming atmosphere runs alongside the counter-culture vibe. They haven't strayed from the heart of Manchester's Northern Quarter though, which has "always been our home" in Dom's words.

With an eye on promoting sustainability, V Rev partnered with Green Earth Appeal to offer Carbon Free Dining, an initiative that plants trees with every meal sold, and offsets the carbon footprint of eating out. They also make sure all takeaway packing and straws are biodegradable and compostable to combat the damage caused by single use plastic.

"I may have started V Rev as an excuse to hang out and listen to punk records while serving food to the occasional customer, but now I get to watch the vegan community boom around us, and strive to make sure our food is at the forefront of the Manchester scene," says Dom. The diner has not only been recognised as the UK's best vegan restaurant at Vegfest 2016, but also as home of the UK's Best Vegan Fried Chicken in the PETA 2018 awards. Dom is very proud of the beef and chicken style burgers made in-house from scratch at the restaurant, and promises that Manchester will certainly see more of V Rev in future: his commitment to great vegan food with a fun side only grows as the restaurant does.

V REV
RANCH DIP

Ranch is one of the most versatile sauces you can make: a creamy, slightly herby sauce that goes well with pretty much anything, and will always see you reaching for more. Dip tenders in it, drizzle it on your pizza, put it in a burger, drink it by the gallon; it's up to you! If you don't have fresh herbs to hand, feel free to use dried as it'll still taste great. Halve the recipe if you're not a glutton for it, but it should hold for a week in the fridge.

1 ½ tbsp finely chopped parsley
1 ½ tbsp finely chopped chives
1 tbsp garlic powder
1 tbsp onion powder
½ tsp black pepper
Pinch of salt
1 ½ tbsp apple cider vinegar
150ml plant milk of your choice
500g vegan mayonnaise

Place all the herbs, seasonings and apple cider vinegar into a blender and blend until you have a smooth paste. Add the plant milk and vegan mayo, and blend till fully incorporated. If you don't have a blender then adding all the ingredients into a bowl and mixing will work; the dip will just have bigger pieces of herbs in. But hey, maybe you prefer that!

If you feel like making this into chipotle ranch dip, substitute the apple cider vinegar for lime juice and add one tinned chipotle pepper and a tablespoon of adobo sauce.

Excellent with our buttermalk fried seitan on the next page.

Preparation time: 5 minutes | Makes 700ml

V REV
BUTTERMALK FRIED SEITAN

This is a fairly involved recipe, but the seitan can be frozen and enjoyed up to a month later. Once you've made the seitan, you can cut it into tenders, nuggets, popcorn-size chunks, etc. and bread it in the same way. Just remember to reduce frying time for smaller sizes.

For the seitan:
500g vital wheat gluten
45g gram (chickpea) flour
30g nutritional yeast
50g chicken-style or vegetable stock powder
½ tsp black pepper
800ml water

For the buttermalk:
250ml soy milk
1 tbsp apple cider vinegar or lemon juice

For the breading:
350g panko breadcrumbs
400g plain flour
10g cayenne pepper
50g garlic powder
40g arrowroot
25g black pepper
25g onion powder
25g salt
20g paprika
10g smoked paprika
10g dried oregano
10g dried parsley

For the seitan

Place all the dry ingredients into a mixing bowl and stir to distribute evenly. Add the water and mix by hand until the dough is a consistent texture. Knead hard for 5 minutes, until the dough is fairly elastic. Bring a large pan of water with the stock to the boil, and then reduce the heat to medium. Cut the dough into eight to ten pieces. Stretch the dough out with your hands to make it as thin as possible. If it tears slightly don't worry, as the dough will expand and fill in any holes while it cooks.

Place the dough pieces in the stock and cook at a gentle simmer. You don't want the stock to boil as it will affect the texture of the seitan, but also make sure it isn't simply poaching. Remove the seitan pieces and place in a container to cool, ensuring that any excess water has been drained off.

For the buttermalk

If you're soy intolerant, you can swap the soy milk for another plant-based milk, but it won't curdle as well and might not coat the seitan as effectively. Mix the milk and apple cider vinegar together in a bowl. Let this stand for 2 minutes and allow the mixture to curdle.

For the breading

We make our breading fairly spicy, so it has more of a Louisiana flavour than Kentucky. If you want less of a kick just reduce or omit the cayenne, and if you like the heat consider adding jalapeno powder to ramp up the impact. Mix all the ingredients thoroughly in a bowl.

Making the fried seitan

Heat oil (vegetable or peanut is best) in your deep fryer or cast iron skillet to around 175°c. While the oil is heating up, bread the seitan by dipping each fillet in the buttermalk, gently shaking off any excess and then coating in breadcrumbs using your other hand. Transfer the breaded fillet back into the buttermalk using your wet hand, shake off the excess again and place it back into the breadcrumbs. Use your dry hand to flip the seitan and check it is evenly coated. Do this with each piece and set aside.

Carefully lower the fillets into the hot oil, being careful not to overcrowd the pan or fryer. Cook for 5 minutes on each side or until golden brown and hot all the way through. Rest on a wire rack above some kitchen roll. Eat hot with ranch dip!

Preparation time: 45 minutes | Cooking time: 20 minutes | Serves: 6-8

A PERFECT

DEAR

A former cheese warehouse in Lancaster is home to not one,
but two longstanding businesses with a unique relationship.

Down an unassuming alley on Penny Street lies a dual institution at the heart of Lancaster's alternative community: The Whale Tail Café and Single Step Wholefoods, a radical meat-free workers' co-op. Ethics are at the heart of everything Single Step does, from the loose goods which enable their customers to purchase plastic-free products to their non-hierarchical structure. Their cosmetics are always environmentally friendly and never tested on animals. Their fresh, organic fruit and veg are as local as seasonally possible and nothing is air freighted.

Established in 1976, Single Step was at the forefront of the plant-based revolution long before the supermarkets jumped on the green bandwagon, and has always remained proudly independent. The shop's name comes from the philosopher Laozi: "A journey of a thousand miles begins with a single step." The team believe that in a consumerist society, global and social change begins with what we put in our shopping baskets. It's these principles which have seen Single Step become an integral part of the town, and for every local yet to discover this hidden gem there's a legion of customers who trek to Lancaster solely to shop before heading upstairs to The Whale Tail...

This comfortable and spacious café is well placed to take advantage of the shop's produce and the two businesses have enjoyed a harmonious and appreciative collaboration for many years. The Whale Tail continues to attract an increasingly wide demographic of customers, including – more than ever – people willing to try our vegetarian and vegan food for the first time. Tricia Rawlinson, the café's owner, adds "We think what makes the Whale Tail special to people is as we try to change and adapt our menu to take advantage of new produce and methods of preparing our food, especially vegan options, we make sure to keep all the much loved, tried and tested favourites on there too. It is very satisfying to still be attracting new customers to the café after more than 25 years in existence, but we never lose touch with our core customer base, many of whom come in most days and have done so right from the start. We have always attracted families to the café and we know many who came in with their children, those children are now all grown up and they come in with their own kids."

The menu is vast and the specials board changes daily. The Whale Tail offers delicious and inspiring soups; healthy salads or poke bowls; burgers galore; curries; tarts and quiches; light and full breakfasts and an amazing selection of vegan cakes and desserts, including their famous vegan chocolate fudge cake and raw, vegan, sugar-free cheesecakes. With a newly refurbished patio garden, the future looks sunny for this much loved café.

Her experience is echoed by the team at Single Step, and everyone is proud of the community feel this engenders, and the strong bond between the two like-minded ventures.

whaletail café

SINGLE STEP

VEGETARIAN   a not-for-profit workers' co-operative   WHOLEFOODS

SPINACH, SWEET POTATO AND CASHEW NUT FILO PIE

This is quite a versatile recipe; you can swap out the sweet potato for regular potato or butternut squash, and if you are not keen on aubergine, courgette works just as well.

For the filling:
400g spinach, washed
300g cashew nuts
1 stick of celery
1 medium-large onion
3 cloves of garlic
600g sweet potato, washed but not peeled
1 large aubergine
4 tbsp olive oil
2 sprigs of rosemary, leaves stripped
Salt and pepper

For the sauce:
50g sunflower margarine/vegan butter
¼ tsp grated nutmeg
40g plain flour
450ml oat milk
10g nutritional yeast
1 tsp stock powder

To assemble:
7 sheets of filo pastry
30g polenta
100ml olive oil
Handful of pumpkin seeds

For the filling

First, preheat a fan oven to 210°c and prepare your ingredients. Wilt the washed spinach by pouring boiling water over it and then refreshing with cold water. Squeeze the spinach to drain off excess water and set aside. Toast the cashews and then blitz slightly in a food processor. Finely dice the celery. Chop the onion, garlic, sweet potato and aubergine into small chunks then transfer to a roasting pan. Drizzle over the four tablespoons of olive oil, scatter over the rosemary leaves, season with salt and pepper, mix well and roast for about 45 to 50 minutes, turning a couple of times. Let the veg cool while you make the sauce.

For the sauce

Heat the margarine or vegan butter in a non-stick pan. Add the nutmeg, some black pepper and the flour. Cook the roux until it goes a little fluffy. Heat the milk in the microwave or a separate pan then gradually stir into the cooked roux. Keep stirring continuously while you add the nutritional yeast and stock powder, then continue to cook for 1 minute.

To assemble

Mix all the prepared ingredients, the roasted veg, and the sauce together. To begin building your pie you will need a deep, rectangular, ovenproof dish about 32 by 25cm. Oil the dish using a pastry brush and line the base with three sheets of filo pastry; the first should overlap the long left hand side of the dish, the next overlap the long right hand side and the third running up the centre to create a firm base. Oil the pastry and sprinkle over a little polenta in between each layer. Spoon the filling into the pie dish, spread it out evenly and repeat with the filo, oil and polenta for two more layers. Next, fold all the overhanging edges of the filo into the centre of the pie to keep the filling in place. Brush with more oil and use up the final two pieces of filo – remembering the oil and polenta in between each layer – to top everything. Finish with a sprinkling of polenta and pumpkin seeds and bake for 30 to 40 minutes in the preheated oven.

Preparation time: 30 minutes | Cooking time: approx. 1 hour 45 minutes | Serves: 6-8

BRANCHING
OUT

The Willow Tree Café is unique for its area thanks to a completely vegan menu which is all made entirely in-house.

Husband and wife Shaun and Stacey established their first ever venture in 2017 and soon gained a social media following and word-of-mouth reputation that put Saltaire straight on the map for vegans. Having worked in a restaurant and as a waitress respectively, when the couple started following a vegan lifestyle they wanted their jobs to reflect more of their personal beliefs and choices. They were also finding it difficult to eat out in Saltaire on a plant-based diet, so the obvious solution presented itself...and, of course, they began their own business!

The Willow Tree Café was initially a pop-up serving vegan food two days a week. Over the next 18 months their feedback and customer base was so positive that it was clearly time to progress to something more permanent, and expand to meet growing demand. The business moved into the empty premises almost opposite their pop-up venue, and has been thriving ever since, providing the kind of comforting food and drink that everyone wants from a neighbourhood hang-out.

"Our aim was always to create a kind of hub where people could eat vegan food without missing out on traditional favourites," says Stacey. "This included

gluten-free vegans as well, as we always have a good few main dishes on and plenty of cakes that anyone can eat." One of The Willow Tree's most popular dishes is the fish and chips, and the big breakfasts tend to go down very well too. Shaun makes the meat alternatives to his own recipe, which the café has become known for and are a staple of the menu. Stacey does all the baking, and also has outside catering on the side.

Between managing, directing, cooking, serving and everything else that comes with running a small independent business, The Willow Tree's co-owners are "very on the go but it's definitely worth it!" They are planning to extend the café into the upstairs space and have recently begun opening for bistro evenings, offering a different menu from the daytime hours and extending the sense of local community even further. "I wanted this to be a warm and friendly place, where you get a greeting as soon as you come in, and you can stay as long as you want," says Stacey. The combination of homemade food and relaxing vibes has proved a big hit, and Saltaire is all the happier for it!

THE WILLOW TREE CAFE

100% plant based food and drinks

STICKY SEITAN 'BEAF' WRAP

This Asian-inspired wrap was developed from our travels in the East.

300g rice
2 spring onions
¼ of a red chilli
Handful of coriander
3 cloves of garlic, peeled
2½ cm piece of ginger, peeled
2 tbsp sesame seeds (optional)
1 tbsp sesame oil
200g seitan strips
60ml soy sauce
¼ of a lime, juiced
2 tbsp brown sugar
10g cornflour
4 tortilla wraps

Rinse the rice until the water runs almost clear, then cover with water and leave to soak for 30 minutes. Boil the water in a pan and then add the soaked rice. Turn down to a simmer and cover with a lid until cooked. Use a fork to fluff the rice up then set aside until ready to assemble the wrap.

Peel the spring onions and slice them diagonally into diamond shapes. Deseed and slice the red chilli (leave the seeds in for extra heat). Tear up the coriander, finely chop the garlic and grate the ginger.

Place a dry pan on the heat, toast the sesame seeds until fragrant then set aside.

To make the filling, heat the sesame oil in a pan and add the seitan. Cook until browned, then add the garlic, ginger and chilli and fry for 1 minute. Add the soy sauce, lime juice, brown sugar and 150ml of water then bring to the boil. Mix the cornflour with 15ml of water to make a slurry, then stir this into the sauce to thicken it.

To assemble the wraps, first spread a quarter (about 75g) of the cooked rice on each wrap, then add some of the sticky seitan 'beaf'. Sprinkle with toasted sesame seeds, spring onion, coriander and extra red chilli if you like. Roll up the wrap, cut in half and you're ready to eat. Enjoy!

KNOW
YOUR ONIONS

Surrounded by the beautiful Yorkshire Wolds, The Yorkshire Wolds Cookery School at Highfield Farm is the perfect place to relax, socialise and most of all improve your cookery skills.

In 2010 a pig farm near the market town of Driffield was converted into the only cookery school in East Yorkshire. As well as the cookery school, Highfield Farm boasts accommodation for up to 18 guests. The carefully renovated farmstead comprises The Yorkshire Wolds Cookery School – which offers a wide range of courses from specialist and guest tutors, including the best-selling author Katy Beskow who teaches vegan cookery and baking – and Highfield Farm Guest Accommodation. From The Duke of Edinburgh's Gold Residential courses to hen parties, the business offers great experiences for beginners, cooking enthusiasts, children, corporate groups and of course anyone interested in learning how to create vegan food at home.

Katy Beskow has been teaching at the school for several years as a guest tutor. The cook and food writer already has three books to her name, and holds a baking class and as well as teaching staple savoury recipes for vegan suppers. Alongside Katy, the regular tutors offer a range of courses including street food, patisserie, sourdough bread, seasonal entertaining…the list is growing, with Nigerian and Lebanese food on the menu for 2019, and guest tutors whose credits include Masterchef, Great British Menu, and Michelin stars regularly hold specialist courses at the school.

The dining room was extended in 2018 and now comfortably seats up to 28 guests with bespoke menus cooked by the school's chefs. Whether it's the ingredients provided for the cookery courses, or the produce used to create delicious meals, the business has a number of local suppliers. The Yorkshire Born and Bred cookery course celebrates ingredients exclusively sourced in 'god's own country' and all the veg used across the business comes from Rafters, a well-established family-run grocer in Driffield.

The Yorkshire Wolds Cookery School and Highfield Farm B&B put quality and friendly people at the heart of everything, thanks to the small but dedicated team who have been there since its very beginnings. Any visit starts with a warm Yorkshire welcome and cake! Each course is an informal, relaxing and skill-building experience and the business as a whole is much more than a cookery school, making the venture unique for the area and an ideal place to try something new or treat yourself!

KATY BESKOW
PUY LENTIL RAGU WITH TAGLIATELLE

Katy Beskow teaches vegan cookery and baking at The Yorkshire Wolds Cookery School, and has created this recipe. Everyone loves a classic ragu, and this vegan version does not disappoint. Most dried pasta sold in supermarkets is vegan, but always check the label to ensure that it is egg-free.

1 tbsp olive oil
1 onion, peeled and finely diced
1 carrot, peeled and finely diced
1 stalk of celery, finely diced
2 cloves of garlic, peeled and crushed
Generous glug of red wine
1 tsp dried mixed herbs
1 tsp dried oregano
400g tinned chopped tomatoes
400g tinned Puy lentils, drained and rinsed
6 cherry tomatoes, quartered
1 tbsp ketchup
140g dried tagliatelle
Drizzle of extra-virgin olive oil
Generous pinch of sea salt and black pepper
Handful of basil leaves, to garnish

In a large pan, heat the olive oil, onion, carrot and celery for 3 to 4 minutes over a medium to high heat, until the vegetables begin to soften. Add the garlic and cook for another minute. Stir in the red wine and herbs then let the liquid reduce for 1 minute. Pour in the chopped tomatoes, Puy lentils, cherry tomatoes and ketchup, then cook for 15 minutes, stirring frequently.

In the meantime, cook the tagliatelle in a pan of simmering water for 8 to 10 minutes until al dente. Thoroughly drain the pasta, then drizzle in some olive oil.

Season the ragu with sea salt and black pepper, then scatter with basil leaves just before serving.

Preparation time: 10 minutes | Cooking time: 30 minutes | Serves 4

DIRECTORY

BUNDOBUST

6 Mill Hill
Leeds
LS1 5DQ
Telephone: 0113 243 1248
Website: www.bundobust.com/leeds
Email: leeds@bundobust.com

61 Piccadilly
Manchester
M1 2AG
Telephone: 0161 359 6757
Website: www.bundobust.com/manchester
Email: manchester@bundobust.com

19 Bold Street
Liverpool
L1 4DN
Website: www.bundobust.com/liverpool
Email: liverpool@bundobust.com
Indian street food and craft beer at several venues across the North.

DANA

214 Crookes Road
Sheffield
S10 1TG
Telephone: 0114 266 6708
Coffee house and vegetarian café with plenty of vegan options in a beautiful and tranquil environment where you can enjoy leisurely lunches, quality coffee and fine teas.

DECKARDS

Currently residing at Barrowboy
453 Abbeydale Road
Sheffield
S7 1FS
Telephone: 07541965313 / 07738993514
Website: www.deckards.co.uk
Street food traders making delicious and exciting food embracing all avenues of culinary styles from around the globe: quality food done in a vibrant and approachable way.

DOWN THE HATCH

62 Duke Street (basement)
Liverpool
L1 5AA
Telephone: 0151 708 0860
Website: www.downthehatchliv.co.uk
*Family-run restaurant with bold burgers and beautiful
bevvies! Ska and reggae music in the background that
keeps heads bopping and faces smiling. Come and see for
yourselves...*

ON THE EIGHTH DAY
CO-OPERATIVE LTD

111 Oxford Road
Manchester
M1 7DU
Telephone: 0161 2734878
Website: www.8thday.coop
*Vegetarian health food shop and café; a business owned
and managed by its workers. A place where you will find
cruelty-free, ethically sourced products, artisan treats and
wholesome, hearty food.*

ELLY JOY

Cutlery Works
73-101 Neepsend Lane
Sheffield
S3 8AT
Website: www.ellyjoy.co.uk
*Elly Joy is a brand creating guilt-free indulgences using
only natural ingredients, making all the products naturally
plant-based, vegan friendly and free from gluten.
Froconut® is our signature soft-serve ice cream alternative
made using coconut milk and coconut water.*

FILMORE AND UNION

Website: www.filmoreandunion.com
Find us on Instagram, Twitter and Facebook @
filmoreandunion
*Yorkshire 'feel good' neighbourhood dining for all with more
than 16 restaurant and cafés across the North. Visit for
breakfast, lunch, Sunday brunch, fresh juicing and organic
coffee.*

GREENS RESTAURANT

43 Lapwing Lane
West Didsbury
Manchester
M20 2NT
Telephone: 0161 434 4259
Website: greensdidsbury.co.uk
*Award-winning neighbourhood restaurant serving quality
vegan and vegetarian cuisine for 28 years with celebrity
chef Simon Rimmer.*

HENDERSON'S
(SHEFFIELD) LTD

2a Parkway Rise
Sheffield
S9 4WQ
Telephone: 0114 242 5724
Website: www.hendersonsrelish.com
*Established in 1885, Henderson's Relish is an iconic
Sheffield sauce, that's still made to a secret recipe known
only to three family members.*

IPPUKU TEA HOUSE

15 Blake Street
York
YO1 8QJ
Telephone: 01904 671311
Website: www.ippukuteahouse.com
*Modern authentic Japanese café and restaurant
specialising in Japanese tea, homemade Japanese food,
cocktails, coffee and homemade cakes. A calm cultural
oasis, open all week.*

JUMPING BEAN

5 Neville Street
Durham
DH1 4EY
Telephone: 07762032223
Website: www.jumpingbeandurham.co.uk
*The first established vegan eatery situated in the heart of
Durham, serving plant-based takes on junk food.*

LEMBAS LTD

The Old Tannery
Unit 5
Whiting Street
Meersbrook
Sheffield
S8 9QR
Telephone: 01142 586 056
Website www.lembas.co.uk
Provider of vegan and vegetarian wholefoods to trade and the public at wholesale prices, delivering across the North of England.

THE LIBRARY CAFÉ & RESTAURANT

10 Leeds Road
Attercliffe
Sheffield
S9 3TY
Telephone: 0114 5538994
Website: www.thelibraryvenue.co.uk
Coffee, kitchen and music housed in the first free library in England dating back to 1894, based in the east end of Sheffield.

LITTLE VEGAN LTD

Unit 1
York Yard
Preston
PR1 1DT
Telephone: 07791980272
Website: www.littlevegan.com
Preston's first completely vegan supermarket, selling founder Carley Stewart's own range of homemade meals alongside goodies from cupboard staples to luxury bodycare, sourced from local vegan producers and suppliers.

MAKE NO BONES

Church: Temple of Fun
4a Rutland Way
Sheffield
S3 8DG
Telephone: 07521610842
Website: www.templeof.fun
100% plant-based vegan kitchen serving bar-food style dishes in our home at Church: Temple of Fun, a completely vegan barcade venue serving up coffees, beers and cocktails. Follow us on Instagram @mnbvegan for more information.

OUR PAULA'S

Chorley
Lancashire
Mobile 07729506553
Email: Ourpaulas@gmail.com
Simply delicious veggie and vegan deli products for everyone to enjoy. Sold at markets and foody events as well as stockist throughout the region, or you can order through the Facebook page – find us @OurPaulas on social media.

OUT OF THIS WORLD

20 New Market Street
Leeds
LS1 6DG
Telephone: 01132 441881
Website: www.outofthisworldonline.com
One-stop shop for the whole spectrum of health foods in a convenient city centre location, stocking organic, eco-friendly, locally-sourced and Fairtrade products.

PJ TASTE LLP

54 Staniforth Road
Sheffield
S9 3HB
Telephone: 0330 0431954
Website: www.pjtaste.co.uk
Delivering delicious and creative food to businesses and individuals across Sheffield and Derbyshire, championing locally grown and seasonal produce.

POM KITCHEN

388 Sharrow Vale Rd
Sheffield
S11 8ZP
Email: pomkitchen@hotmail.com
Aussie-inspired veggie and vegan eatery.

POUR

617 London Road
Sheffield
S2 4HT
Website: www.poursheffield.co.uk
Email: info@poursheffield.co.uk
Craft beer and pizza, dog friendly, vegan with vegetarian options.

PRASHAD

137 Whitehall Road
Drighlington
BD11 1AT
Telephone: 01132852037
Website: www.prashad.co.uk
Family-run restaurant serving contemporary Indian vegetarian cuisine.

SHED 100% PLANT-BASED CAFÉ

Cutlery Works
73-101 Neepsend Lane
Sheffield
S3 8AT
Website: www.Eatshed.com
Find us on Facebook and instagram @eatshed
Our 100% plant-based café boasts some of the most healthful eats in town, including our tempting signature hot dishes, breakfast burritos, build-your-own bowls, cakes, power bars, smoothies, cold-pressed juices and more.

SHOE TREE CAFÉ

150 Heaton Park Road
Newcastle upon Tyne
NE6 5NR
Find us on Facebook and Instagram @shoetreecafe
Relaxed and friendly vegan and veggie café serving decent grub and delicious drinks as well as hosting workshops and events.

SINGLE STEP WHOLEFOODS

78a Penny Street
Lancaster
LA1 1XN
Telephone: 01524 63021
Website: www.singlestep.org.uk
A meat-free worker's co-op providing Lancaster with organic wholefoods since 1976.

SOUTH STREET KITCHEN

19-20 South Street
Park Hill
Sheffield
S2 5QX
Telephone: 07763 678858
Website: www.southstreetkitchen.org
Laid-back and sustainable café for the local community serving vibrant Middle Eastern flavours in a bright, welcoming space on Sheffield's iconic Park Hill estate.

SUNSHINE DELI

989 Penistone Road
Sheffield
S6 2DH
Telephone: 07510596159
E-mail: SunshineDeli1@outlook.com
Totally plant-based goodness in the form of healthy, traditional and comfort food from the deli as well as catering, deliveries and events.

THE TASTY VEGAN FOOD COMPANY

Whitburn
Sunderland
Telephone: 07471 685 325
Email: info@tastyveganfood.co.uk
Website: www.tastyveganfood.co.uk
Vegan cakes and catering, supplying cafés across the north and also available to private customers. More importantly, food made with love and positivity!

TYNE CHEASE

42 Cade Hill Road
Stocksfield
NE43 7PU
Website: www.tynechease.com
Email: info@tynechease.com
Small family-run business producing a unique range of award-winning artisanal vegan cheese, which can be found online and at vegan festivals all over the North.

UNICORN GROCERY

89 Albany Road
Chorlton
M21 0BN
Telephone: 0161 861 0010
Website: www.unicorn-grocery.coop
Workers' co-operative offering its Manchester customer base an unbeatable range of affordable, fresh and wholesome food with an emphasis on organic, fair-trade and local produce.

V REV VEGAN DINER

20-26 Edge Street
Manchester
M4 1HN
Telephone: 0161 806 0928
Website: www.vrevmcr.co.uk
Vegan junk food diner located in the heart of the Northern Quarter, serving plant based beef burgers, fried seitan chicken, huge milkshakes, cocktails and much more.

VEGANNOMNOMS PRESTON

24 Garden Walk
Ashton
Preston
PR2 1DP
Telephone: 07779779662
Email: vegannomnomspreston@gmail.com
Website: www.vegannomnomspreston.co.uk
Small business all about delicious vegan food, including cakes to order, flexible catering for any occasion and a monthly Secret Supper Club.

WAPENTAKE

92 Kirkgate
Leeds
LS2 7DJ
Telephone: 0113 243 6248
Website: www.wapentakeleeds.co.uk
'A Little Piece of Yorkshire' with brunch and hearty classics on the menu, including vegan alternatives for every option.

THE WHALE TAIL CAFÉ

78a Penny Street
Lancaster
LA1 1XN
Telephone: 01524 845133
Website: www.whaletailcafe.co.uk
Exclusively vegan and vegetarian café in a converted city centre warehouse, featuring a beautiful, secluded patio garden.

THE WILLOW TREE CAFÉ

93 Kirkgate
Shipley
West Yorkshire
BD18 3LR
Telephone: 01274 013170
Website: www.thewillowcafesaltaire.co.uk
Relaxed and welcoming café serving a completely vegan menu, all freshly made, from traditional favourites like fish and chips to big breakfasts and gluten-free cakes.

THE YORKSHIRE WOLDS COOKERY SCHOOL

Highfield Farm
Southburn
Driffield
YO25 9AF
Telephone: 01377 270607
Website: www.yorkshirewoldscookeryschool.co.uk
One of kind cookery school for the area, proudly supporting local producers and providing high quality facilities to offer a wide range of classes combined with a true Yorkshire welcome.

OTHER TITLES AVAILABLE

The Little Book of Cakes & Bakes

Featuring recipes and stories from the kitchens of some of the nation's best bakers and cake-makers.
978-1-910863-48-0

Plant Milk Power

How to create your own delicious, nutritious and nourishing moo-free milks and smoothies.
978-1-910863-41-1

Tasty & Healthy

Eating well with lactose intolerance, coeliac disease, Crohn's disease, ulcerative colitis and irritable bowel syndrome.
978-1-910863-36-7

In Their Footsteps

Celebrating 25 years of baking at Jervaulx Abbey.
978-1-910863-37-4

Sweet Chilli Friday

Simple vegetarian recipes from our kitchen to yours.
978-1-910863-38-1

TITLES FROM OUR 'GET STUCK IN' SERIES

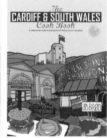

The Edinburgh and East Coast Cook Book

features Masterchef winner Jamie Scott at The Newport, Fhior, Pickering's Gin, Pie Not, Stockbridge Market and much more.
978-1-910863-45-9

The Glasgow and West Coast Cook Book

features The Gannet, Two Fat Ladies, The Spanish Butcher, Hutchesons City Grill, Gamba and much more.
978-1-910863-43-5

The Manchester Cook Book: Second Helpings

features Ben Mounsey of Grafene, Hatch, Refuge, Masons, Old School BBQ Bus and much more.
978-1-910863-44-2

The Derbyshire Cook Book: Second Helpings

features Chris Mapp at The Tickled Trout, Chatsworth Farm Shop, Michelin-starred Fischer's, Peacock and much more.
978-1-910863-34-3

The Cardiff & South Wales Cook Book

features James Sommerin of Restaurant James Sommerin, Cocorico Patisserie, Sosban and much more.
978-1-910863-31-2

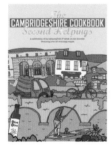

The Cambridgeshire Cook Book: Second Helpings

features Mark Abbott of Midsummer House, The Olive Grove, Elder Street Café and much more.
978-1-910863-33-6

The Lakes & Cumbria Cook Book

features Simon Rogan's L'Enclume, Forest Side, Hawkshead Relish, L'al Churrasco and much more.
978-1-910863-30-5

The Nottingham Cook Book: Second Helpings

features Welbeck Estate, Memsaab, Sauce Shop, 200 Degrees Coffee, Homeboys, Rustic Crust and lots more.
978-1-910863-27-5

The South London Cook Book

features Jose Pizzaro, Adam Byatt from Trinity, Jensen's Gin, LASSCO, Salt and Pickle, Chadwicks and much more.
978-1-910863-27-5

The Essex Cook Book

features Daniel Clifford, Thomas Leatherbarrow, The Anchor Riverside, Great Garnetts, Deersbrook Farm, Mayfield Bakery and much more.
978-1-910863-25-1

All our books are available from Waterstones, Amazon and good independent bookshops.

Find out more about us at www.mezepublishing.co.uk